Praise for

"An ambitious and triumphar
building a house to marrying
daughter she never met—to w...
forgiveness. It is a story of leaps of faith and second chances, and ...
your heart up to the brim."

—Sharon Harrigan, author of *Playing with Dynamite* and *Half*

"In this beautifully crafted memoir full of rich, sensory imagery, Carole Duff takes readers with her on her dangerous yet healing journey of growth and faith in her maturing season. This book will speak tenderly to those building a second marriage, those seeking purpose after closing the book of a long career, and those wrestling with shame and God's gentle whisper to 'leave it.'"

—Afton Rorvik, author of *Living Connected: An Introvert's Guide to Friendship* and *Storm Sisters: Friends Through All Seasons*

"*Wisdom Builds Her House* is a captivating memoir that delves into the profound themes of searching, and finding, grace, mercy, and wisdom. Written with heartfelt sincerity, Carole Duff takes us on an inspiring and deeply personal odyssey through her life's most profound moments, revealing a narrative filled with spiritual awakening and transformative experiences. This entrancing narrative is a testament to the resilience of the human spirit, and a reminder that 'some truths can only be seen in darkness.'"

—Lisa St. John, author of *Swallowing Stones*

"A moving story of family trauma, childhood secrets, and the author's attempt to reconcile faith with her deeply ingrained expectations of perfection. Duff invites the reader on her truth-seeking and as witness to the building of her literal and spiritual house. The beautiful writing drew me in and the story kept me engaged."

—Karen DeBonis, author of *Growth: A Mother, Her Son, and the Brain Tumor They Survived*

"Carole Duff's memoir is the unflinchingly honest story of her leaving a productive teaching career, overseeing the building a physical home, and delving into her past to find the freedom to go forward. It's the story of important internal work, inspired by her stepdaughter's journals and led by the Holy Spirit to find the place where Wisdom has built her house."

—Judy Allen, author of *Reimagining Retirement* on Substack

"Never has a book title been more aptly chosen, for those four words encapsulate Carole's outward experiences, and ultimately more significantly, her inner refinement. This is a powerful story of sanctification, an exposé of *being* triumphing over *doing*, a testimony of godly becoming—for it is in becoming that wisdom is built."

—Rachel Campbell, MA (Theology), UK-based Christian writer and speaker

"Through laying the foundation, framing, and shaping her new home on a mountaintop hillside, Carole Duff simultaneously unpacks and dismantles a

lifetime of ghosts in the closet in hopes of finally building that one safe place for herself and her new husband. With strength, honesty, and bravery, Duff makes her way into the past to know herself better and find herself in the tender love of the One who knows us fully."
—Sarah M. Wells, author of *American Honey: A Field Guide to Temptation*

"The fabric of this story is dense and sure, drawn together as it is into the metaphor of the wisdom house. Duff's honest and self-aware voice, along with her wonderfully descriptive scenes make this book a pleasure to read and a challenge to all of us: would we be able, as Duff is, to be as honest in the building of our own wisdom houses?"
—Carol D. Marsh, author of *Nowhere Else I Want to Be*

"Though already walking a spiritual path, Carole Duff dives deeper into a lifelong habit of prayerful questioning when she discovers the young adult journals of her husband's dead daughter. With the young woman's candid voice echoing through the narrative, her questions force Duff to confront realities of her own existence as a mother, a daughter, and a woman all too familiar with fear. When women join forces to ask questions, even in these unusual circumstances—separated by time, generations, and death—Duff's story reminds us that within this mutuality and connection lies the brave work of transformation."
—Suzanne Ohlmann, author of *Shadow Migration: Mapping a Life*

"There is a refreshing depth to Carole's writing. As she so poignantly describes, one's childhood experiences affect all of life, but with God's subtle guidance, even the difficult ones can be a source of insight and growth."
—Rev. Dr. David J. Ludwig, pastor, professor emeritus in psychology, licensed therapist, author, and international speaker

"In a rare exposition of intentional personal and spiritual reflection and growth, Carole Duff unfolds a tale of challenges and achievements. This is a fascinating book, and an inspiring one. Those who believe that the examined life is the one most worth living will admire the author's hard work, insights, curiosity, and courage."
—Irene Hoge Smith, author of *The Good Poetic Mother*

"In Carole Duff's *Wisdom Build Her House*, one can almost hear the voices, watch the action, and feel the powerful emotions of the protagonist journeying through her relationship with God, her husband, daughter, stepdaughter (via her journal), and pastor—to find 'freedom' at last."
—Dr. Marti Brueggeman, author of
The Ever After Life of the Brothers Grimm Fairy Tales

"After years of self-doubt and inner-criticism manifesting in perfectionism and the relentless pursuit to do more, Carole Duff senses a prompting from the Spirit to wait. Carving out space and time for inner work, she learns to face her fears and shine a light on long-kept secrets, landing in a place of renewal and freshness in her faith. Her story will resonate with anyone who

has ever tried to earn a place at the table by doing more before realizing that embracing our 'being' self is the key to healing, wisdom, and a deeper faith."
—Linda Hoye, author of *The Presence of Absence:
A Story About Busyness, Brokenness, and Being Beloved*

"Scaffolding the story around the physical construction of the house where they plan to settle into their next phase of life, Carole Duff courageously guides her reader through the metaphorical deconstruction of her past—finally confronting long-buried experiences of trauma, fear, shame, guilt, and spiritual discontent—in order to rebuild her sense of self and faith into a structure that is solid and lasting. *Wisdom Builds Her House* is a hopeful testament to the fact that it's never too late to navigate our way to personal and familial healing."
—Melanie Brooks, author of *A Hard Silence*

WISDOM
Builds Her House

Carole Duff

Brandylane
Publishers, Inc.
Publishing books since 1985

Copyright © 2024 by Carole Duff

All rights reserved. No part of this book may be reproduced in any form or by any electronic or mechanical means, or the facilitation thereof, including information storage and retrieval systems, without permission in writing from the publisher, except in the case of brief quotations published in articles and reviews. Any educational institution wishing to photocopy part or all of the work for classroom use, or individual researchers who would like to obtain permission to reprint the work for educational purposes, should contact the publisher.

ISBN: 978-1-962416-04-7
Library of Congress Control Number: 2023918698

Designed by Sami Langston
Production management by Maryanna Stufflebeem

Printed in the United States of America

Published by
Brandylane Publishers, Inc.
5 S. 1st Street
Richmond, Virginia 23219

brandylanepublishers.com

For Keith and our daughters

Contents

Part I: Building the House

1. Gretchen's Journals 1
2. No Attic, Few Closets 7
3. House Site 11
4. Design 16
5. Financing 20
6. The Basement 26
7. House Framing 32
8. Under Roof 37
9. Appliances 41
10. Paint Colors 45
11. Flooring 49
12. Accessories 53

Part II: Moving to Vanaprastha

13. Re-missioning 59
14. Anniversaries 64
15. Two Professions 69
16. A Third Way 75
17. No Accident 79
18. Star Trails 84
19. The Secret 88
20. Mothers and Daughters 94
21. Four Houses 100
22. Mistakes Were Made 105
23. Freya Joins the Pack 111
24. Unsettled 116
25. Untrusting 120
26. Fathers and Daughters 125
27. Seeking the Truth 131
28. Wednesday, March 27, 1957 136

29. The Real Secret 141
30. Both Sinner and Saint 146

Part III: Finding Grace

31. At War 153
32. Selfies 158
33. Trust Tests 162
34. Steps Forward and Back 166
35. Both-And Teachers 170
36. Gretchen's Goodbye 175
37. The Comfort of Guilt 182
38. Still the Laundry 187
39. I am Powerless 193
40. Freedom 199
Acknowledgements 205
Discussion Questions 207
About the Author 209

Part I: Building the House

Wisdom has built her house, she has hewn her seven pillars.
She has slaughtered her animals, she has mixed her wine, she has also set her table.
She has sent out her servant-girls, she calls from the highest places in the town,
"You that are simple, turn in here!" To those without sense she says,
"Come, eat of my bread and drink of the wine I have mixed.
Lay aside immaturity, and live, and walk in the way of insight."

Proverbs 9:1-6 (NRSV)

Chapter 1

Gretchen's Journals

I found them by chance in our Alexandria townhouse while cleaning closets during spring break. Keep. Pitch. Give away. That Friday morning, I walked into her sun-yellow room, which my husband Keith had converted into a study, and slid open the mirrored closet doors. As I reached for an open crate on the floor, I knew immediately. Except for Keith's stories, this was all that was left of his fierce yet soft-spoken daughter. I dropped to my knees and touched Gretchen's things. Her gold high school class ring with a sapphire blue stone. Her black, 24 by 20-inch professional art portfolio with carrying handle. Her green writing journal with a Rousseau primitive on the cover. I pulled my hand away, stepped back, and closed the closet door.

Keith didn't mention Gretchen often, though he seemed to enjoy talking about her whenever he did. I'd learned to curb my impulse to interrupt and bide my time. So, when Keith got home from work, I waited until he'd changed his clothes, made his end-of-the-week Martini, and settled into his recliner in the living room.

"I found Gretchen's things today," I said. "While cleaning upstairs. She kept a journal."

He took a sip of his Martini. "Gretchen told me she wanted to tell herself the truth. In her teen years, she noticed how different events and feelings were from her memories of them, even recent memories. I encouraged her to write things down when they happened, to keep a journal so she could see how her thinking changed." His intense blue eyes fixed on me as I stirred a pot of homemade spaghetti sauce in the open galley kitchen. "Alex read them, I haven't, but we talked about what she wrote, so I don't think I will." Alex was Gretchen's younger brother.

WISDOM BUILDS HER HOUSE

The aroma of the deep red sauce—tomato, garlic, onion, parsley, plus cinnamon, nutmeg, and cloves to heighten flavor—filled the kitchen. "Would it be okay if I read them?" I asked then waited, giving his analytical mind time to process his feelings.

"Oh yes." Keith leaned forward and smiled. "Reading my daughter's journal is the best way to get to know her. And you can ask me anything you'd like."

Being a historian, I welcomed his invitation to learn about his daughter and share our pasts with one another. Except. Earlier that same week, in my own closet, I'd found three plastic shopping bags stuffed with letters I'd written to my parents, starting when I left home for college. Mother had kept my letters over the years, and my sisters sent them to me after clearing her attic a month ago, part of a failed attempt to move Mother to a safer place. I'd shoved the bags of letters to the back of my closet.

Dipping a teaspoon into the spaghetti sauce, I blew on the sample and tasted. Perfect.

"I never kept a journal," I said. "But I wrote letters to my parents twice each week for thirty years. After my father died, I emailed or called Mother every day, same as now."

"Letters and emails are less honest than a journal, a step away from the truth, like secondary sources." Keith was a history major, too.

My hackles rose. "I suppose."

Why didn't he appreciate how dutiful I was? Was he saying his daughter was better than me? More honest? More loved?

I pursed my lips. What *was* in her journal? I decided to find out during my next break from work, our Fourth of July vacation at Blackwater Falls in West Virginia.

We rented a small, rustic one-room cabin—a quiet forest retreat like the mountain house we planned to build—and packed a week of supplies. The first morning, in chill and drizzle, we hiked the muddy trails among rhododendrons in late bloom—quiet "God time," a prayerful listening-while-walking exercise I'd done every day since becoming a believer in my early forties. As we listened to the sounds of God's creation, a loamy scent arose from the earth, and forest leaves bowered our path. Keith and I threw sticks for Heathcliff, the one-year-old, hundred-pound, black lab mix the two of us had adopted from the Alexandria Shelter the previous fall. Heathcliff barked and chased and chewed.

Back at the cabin, we sipped our coffee beside the hearth fire. I cooked eggs-over-easy: whites shimmering with a dusting of salt and pepper, yokes unbroken and runny when forked. Just the way Keith liked them.

After breakfast, Keith read by the fire while I stacked Gretchen's journals on the nightstand beside the queen-sized bed, the only "sofa" in the small, one-room cabin. I switched on the lamp, propped the bed pillows, and ordered the journals by the opening date. Six, 9 by 6-inch books, ranging from February 1996 to June 2001: a black plastic spiral, the green Rousseau print, then four hardcovers. Donning my reading glasses, I opened her first book.

> **February 25, 1996**: "I wonder, will I be honest with my observations, or will I edit my life self-consciously, knowing I'll have witnesses? Or one witness. I don't know. Please, don't be angry with me."

Her words flowed in small, neat pencil-print free of erasures, unlike my college letters' sloppy penmanship and disorganized after-thoughts dancing up the sides and onto the envelope. They also cut to the core: she was so insightful she'd even questioned her own honesty. Neat, self-aware, and smart. Gretchen had been a National Merit Commended Scholar, like my older sister, and a scholarship recipient in creative writing.

I adjusted my glasses and focused on Gretchen's question about witnesses. She had written for herself and expected to have readers; now I was among them. Mid-way through the first journal, I discovered who her other witnesses had been.

> **June 5, 1998**: "I have this habit of measuring time in lovers, in men and women I've kept time with, made time with. It always seems like the most natural step to say, I like you, I may love you; we should go to bed in order to find out."

I squirmed at such an intimate admission. Did Keith know about this—her seemingly unrestrained, sexual pleasure-seeking? I pushed the book aside.

The second book contained more entries from 1996 plus stories and poems, both copied and original like this:

> *I maintained a safe distance*
> *But I'm crippled somehow.*

Safe distance. I rocked my head from left to right. Of course, she'd want to protect herself from those who might wish to hurt her. *Crippled somehow.* How many times in childhood had I declared, "I am not a cripple," while pointing to my clubfoot? But I knew her word "crippled" had nothing to do with a surgically repaired clubfoot.

This wasn't getting easier. I shook my head to banish those thoughts and placed the second book on top of the first.

I opened the third book and skimmed through duplicate poems and entries until this.

> **August 17, 1998:** "What a nice party this weekend! I was able to get ridiculously drunk and still have a fun time... everything I looked at was flipping in front of my eyes like a television with poor reception. Ah, beer. Also, I sucked down some excellent Merlot..."

Gretchen drank a lot—I heard the hard-edged voice of my inner judge. In my head, the scene switched from her college years to mine. There I was, slim and shapely in a miniskirt, a shy, mousy-brown-long-haired, good girl at a mixer, circling the edge of the dance floor. I envied the flashy fast girls getting all the dances and dates. My smile masked self-righteousness, disdain, jealousy, and fear that no one would ask me to dance—or maybe it hadn't.

Forty years separated then and now, most of those years spent parenting two children and teaching history to adolescent girls. I didn't want to think about my past, so I swallowed the bad feelings. My gut churned, releasing a surge of anger to my brain, as memories of my daughter Jessica's teenage behavior stirred. The shame that followed reminded me of who I had been—a mother who'd failed to stay calm when Jessica needed me the most.

"Oh, for goodness sake, Carole," I muttered to myself. "Angry with a dead girl, and after she asked you not to be?"

I wasn't proud of these thoughts. Part of me felt guilty for having them, and the other part felt perfectly justified. People are responsible for their actions and should think before they act. Right?

"Darn," I growled through clenched teeth, sealing my lips so Keith wouldn't hear. The honesty in Gretchen's journals was bringing out the worst in me, qualities I worked hard to hide. What had I been thinking, taking the journals on vacation? What had I expected, a beach read? Instead of facing those questions, I did what I usually do: ignore them and forge ahead.

The fourth book.

> **March 7, 1999:** "I checked everything out with a hand mirror in the bathroom. The virus had gotten so much worse; it was horrifying to see myself eaten up with this shit from the inside out. I began shrieking and threw the mirror at the wall…"

Then the fifth.

> **June 7, 2000:** "Who do you know that you'd trust not only with your house when you're gone, but also with your corpse when you're dead?"

Then the sixth.

> **January 8, 2001:** "I ran the hot water in the sink, pulled up a chair, drained a couple of beers and began to slice. I couldn't find a vein…"

I imagined Gretchen falling down a deep, dark well and me falling with her. "Help me, because I can't help myself," she wrote. In my head, I heard another cry, one from a vivid dream I'd had since childhood. "Help, please, please help." The nightmare, absent for more than a decade, had returned. My hands stretched out, as if I could reach through the pages of her journal and save her. But my nightmare and Gretchen's story always ended the same way. Her final journal slipped from my fingers and crashed onto the cabin floor.

Keith looked up from his reading. "Are you all right?"

My hand shook as I retrieved the fallen book. "Uh-huh, but this is tough going."

"Yes. I know. I lived it."

With that, I closed the journal and returned her books to the crate. The questions her writings provoked were far too big for me to resolve in one week. Yes, Keith knew about this. And I was unable to abide with him emotionally.

While carrying the crate out to the car, I wondered what would happen if I maintained a safe distance from all of this. The answer was immediate and unequivocal: I would be less of a person—crippled, and my marriage, too. I remembered an old Chinese proverb: Go into the heart of danger, for there you will find safety. Perhaps by reading Gretchen's journals and delving into the past, I would find what I longed for. Not so much safety but freedom. Freedom from fear.

Then and there, I made a firm promise: to read the journals of a young woman I'd never met, a girl who had ended her life at age twenty-four, a daughter in some ways similar to my own. To read all six books, every word from the beginning to the end, after I resigned my long-distance job the following year.

Unbeknownst to me, this was the beginning of a seven-year journey, which would indeed lead me into the heart of danger. There I would find safety for the first time in my life.

Chapter 2

No Attic, Few Closets

July 1, 2010. While merging into a swirl of traffic on the Baltimore Beltway at Providence Road, my final commute home, I thought about the decision I'd made. I had given up my job, which entailed staying with a colleague during the week, so Keith and I could live together for the first time in our four-year marriage. We were building a new house, a mountain chalet with no attic and few closets, in preparation for the third stage of life.

While passing the next exit—Dulaney Valley Road to Hampton Lane, the alternate route to the school where I had taught—I felt a heaviness in my chest. A more honest reason for my resignation was, though the passion still burned, I no longer had the patience for teaching. The same had happened with my other profession: parenting. When I accepted the job in Maryland eight years before, I'd sold my house in Texas, packed my son off to college, and drove away, leaving my twenty-two-year-old, college-graduated daughter behind. I'd lost patience with that work, too, and I was tired. And yet, I mourned the loss of the work-and-kids life that had brought joy.

While my brain wrestled with that tension, I went deep into my heart and prayed.

I know this is what you want me to do, but without teaching or parenting, I don't know who I am anymore or what I'm called to do.

I'd been talking with God every day since my first marriage failed and I'd given up atheism. For twenty years, the Spirit's gentle voice had guided me through endings and beginnings like this one. My new job would be housewife, finance manager, and overseer of construction for our forest retreat in the Blue Ridge Mountains.

"Will house-building be enough?" I asked myself—and God. How small that question sounds to me now. How big the answer turned out to be.

I heard a high-pitched roar and glanced into the rearview mirror. A speeding motorcyclist was swerving through the heavy traffic. When he pulled behind my car, I noticed his torn jeans and short-sleeved shirt. The tinted visor of his helmet hid his face. I eased up on the accelerator, hoping the young man would pass before the 83 exchange.

He revved his engine and pulled within inches of my back bumper. Three more quick revs drew him closer. I gripped the steering wheel and pressed my back into the seat's lumbar support. Why me? With so many cars on the road, why was he threatening me? Looking for an escape, I calculated the other vehicles' potential moves and countermoves against my own. But, like a player stalemated in chess, I was out of options.

Game over?

Time stopped. Except for the motorcyclist and engine roar, all sound and imagery faded. I felt a gentle breeze and calmed. Will I die here on the Baltimore Beltway before my second half of life begins? Another question surfaced. Would dying be easier than facing the future? And then this: Am I any different from this unknown man, racing forward and putting the past behind him, regardless of the consequences?

Adrenaline spiked through my body.

Immediately, time resumed. The cyclist sliced left and shot past, weaving around vehicles like a video game avatar. Part of me admired his skill and envied the freedom his ease suggested. Another part felt guilty for having those feelings. To hide the guilt, I chose my default.

"Fool." I ground my teeth and glared.

As the motorcycle disappeared into the distance and the roar died away, I put the incident out of my mind, including the time lapse. But later—more than three years later—there would come a moment when I'd recall the scene in vivid detail and note how it aligned with an event from my distant past. Meanwhile, like the Hebrews wandering in the wilderness for forty years before crossing into the Promised Land, I would stand at that dangerous threshold.

Until I remembered.

Keith and I were aware of the risks in building a new house, both the physical structure and the metaphor. Not a first half of life do-over but a second half of life do-differently, together. We had both failed in previous marriages, though I will only speak of my own. Mine had made perfect sense. My first husband was a university professor, like my father, and not a believer, also like my father. Tall and slim. Like my father. Yet our sixteen-year marriage ended when he moved out, leaving me feeling rejected, ashamed, and alone. My worst fears had come true.

That midlife failure had placed me at a crossroad. With encouragement from believing friends, I gave up forty years of I'm-too-smart-to-believe-in-God atheism. My two children and I visited a church near the school where I taught in Dallas, sang in the choirs, and were baptized so we could become members. Then, after Jessica and David graduated from college and high school, respectively, I moved to the new job in Baltimore and seven months later met and fell in love with a man from Virginia.

But marrying Keith did not make perfect sense. Marriage meant selling the house I'd purchased, moving into his Alexandria townhouse, getting to know each other's grown children, tending to our aging parents, and giving up my job—all while preparing for retirement, together. And Keith, less-than-average in height and built solid, looked nothing like my father.

Exiting the Baltimore Beltway at 95-south, continuing the sixty-mile drive through Maryland and Washington D.C., I rubbed the back of my neck. Wouldn't it have been easier to remain single, live in my own house, and work until I died? Maybe, but hadn't I made those decisions already? Besides, as with the last move, I had faith in God and the Spirit's guidance—as did Keith. Yet, I knew our four-year "honeymoon" of weekends and vacations was ending, and the true tests of marriage lay ahead, including the secrets hiding in our closets.

The new Wilson Bridge rose so far above the Potomac I couldn't see the dangerous currents below as I could when crossing the old bridge. I found the blindness both comforting and disconcerting. Ambivalence either way.

Crossing into Virginia, I thought about another decision I'd made: to assume primary responsibility for Heathcliff. To my mind, Heathcliff wasn't all that different from an adolescent who needed consistent rules applied without fail. While I understood this as a teacher of adolescent girls, I had to admit my lack of success with this approach while trying to guide my daughter Jessica during her turbulent years. Not knowing the reason for my inconsistency still troubled our relationship—something else in my rearview mirror. I hoped working with Heathcliff would provide some insight and give me something else to do to fill my time.

I pulled into a reserved space in the parking lot and headed to our townhouse. Heathcliff greeted me with hops, grins, snorts, and tail wags. I stroked his velvet-soft ears.

"Good boy, Heathcliff, good boy. I'm home." Home to walk him. Home to build a house with Keith. Home to read Gretchen's journals and sort through the stuff in my closet.

I figured it would take about a year to train Heathcliff, get to know Gretchen, and resolve the questions her life provoked in me—the same amount of time for completing our mountain house—then life would go on. I'd go back to teaching. Or something. The vagueness surrounding "or something" provoked a deep disquiet I hadn't felt in a long time.

So, I focused on the present mission: to build a house with no attic and few closets. Little did I know what I would encounter along the way.

Chapter 3

House Site

The air-conditioner compressor rattled against the summer heat. Heathcliff and I pressed our noses against the glass storm door, watching Keith back out of the parking lot and head to his job as a respected, in-demand intelligence analyst contracted to the government. After he drove off, I shut the solid security door behind me. Day one.

Not retirement. A *sabbatical*. That's what I called my chosen unemployment at age fifty-eight. After four decades of uninterrupted paychecks, I feared not making money, which I saw as a powerful symbol of independence and measure of my worth. Though Keith had encouraged me, I fought the change because I worried about relying on someone else, having misjudged before, and because of my father's experience during his own sabbatical. Without daily reminders of who he was, a professor of pediatrics, my father lost direction. His tall, beanpole body wandered the house in brown fleece-lined slippers and maroon sweats. I was afraid the wandering might happen to me, too, because I shared his affliction, though I hadn't had an episode of depression in years. As long as I kept busy, I felt confident I could outrun it.

I made a list of what needed to be done to get our house built. Secure a construction loan qualified for rollover to a conventional loan. Communicate with loan officers, bankers, and the attorney. Coordinate with the builder. Since we'd started the process six months ago—collaborating with designers, hiring a contractor, paying for the house site's rough-in driveway, applying for the loan—housebuilding was already my part-time job.

Other to-dos crowded my sabbatical's checklist. Watch over my widowed eighty-seven-year-old mother who lived alone in Connecticut, try new things, read all the books I'd promised I would get to someday, walk and train Heathcliff.

Get to know Gretchen. Figure out who I am now.

That first morning, when not on the phone or emailing our bankers, builder, or attorney, I returned to the promise I'd made the previous year. Gretchen and those unsettling questions raised in her journals. "Ask me anything you'd like," Keith had said. He also gave me full access to his files—all of them—anything in the house. "No secrets."

Maybe if I uncovered the secrets in his daughter's closet, I'd find the courage to face those in mine. That was the point, the why, and I would discover, my biggest challenge.

Before diving into the journals, I asked myself what I knew about Gretchen's childhood. I opened my laptop and started another list. Born on the Autumnal Equinox of the Bicentennial year, her younger brother Alex born less than two years later. Precocious: her mind grew faster than her body, only five feet and one hundred pounds as an adult; read to herself at age three; at four taught Alex to read and showed interest in drawing, which led to a profession in art. Physically fearless: riding bikes, jumping off the high dive at the community pool to learn how to swim, kicking through the board at Tae Kwon Do trials when no one else did. Child of divorce: her parents separated when she was five. For ten years, she and Alex lived with their mother. Then, as teenagers, they moved in with Keith and called the townhouse home until they left for college. Gretchen's journals began in the middle of her freshman year of college. I saved the document, reached for her first book, and read the first entry again.

> **February 25, 1996**: "I wonder, will I be honest with my observations, or will I edit my life self-consciously, knowing I'll have witnesses? Or one witness. I don't know... I worry I'm not deserving of trust..."

Later, I would read that her "one witness" was a boyfriend who read her journal on occasion. Now, I was the one witness, and trust was the question.

Trust. I bookmarked my place and pondered. Certainly, I was trustworthy at work, a good hard worker as Gretchen had been, according to Keith. But she wasn't referring to work ethics; she meant deserving of trust from those with whom she'd been sexually intimate if not emotionally honest. In a perfect world, love and trust merged into one, what Gretchen called "Merged Permanence." Was I worthy of that kind of trust? A question I'd never asked because I wanted the answer to be yes. Absolutely yes. I rubbed my face. Deep down I knew the answer wasn't so simple. And deeper down I feared the answer might be maybe.

Or no.

Intuitive and resolute by nature, Keith expressed confidence in us from the beginning of our relationship, trusting me from the start. His marriage proposal on our fourth date left me speechless. I answered yes, an uncharacteristically impulsive decision yet practical given the traffic-clogged commute between my home north of Baltimore and his in Alexandria, south of D.C. We agreed to a long engagement and, after marriage, to build a house together.

With Gretchen's journal still in hand, I remembered the Saturday morning in the spring of 2003 when Keith first brought me to his sixteen forested acres in Virginia's Blue Ridge, two months after we'd met and a month after he proposed. We forged a path through the dense woods, winding upward, skirting rock outcroppings and stands of mountain laurel blooming pink and white. Keith led the way, holding low branches away from our faces. Massive sentinel oaks, spared from lumbering a hundred years ago, spread their lofty branches like cathedrals with vaulted arches, sheltering an abundance of life: mammals, reptiles, birds, and insects.

I scampered along, my backpack filled with garden gloves, a trowel, and narcissus bulbs. On steep inclines, our feet slid on layers of dry leaf-litter carpeting the forest floor, and we skidded several feet down the mountain. Both of us recovered quickly, though soil stained our hands and dampened the knees of our pants.

Is this what you want me to do? I prayed while climbing, skidding, and recovering. *Can I trust my heart this time?*

We reached the first plateau, a shelf of land, which would be the house site. Glancing at Keith, I wondered if he had doubts about our metaphorical housebuilding. I had doubts—about me, not him.

Breathing hard and sweating, I lifted my face into the mountain breeze and looked west, back across the Rockfish Valley to the Blue Ridge Mountains and the Three Ridges Wilderness Area. Chickadees flitted among the slender mast-tall tulip poplars which had reforested the land. Red-tailed hawks and golden eagles floated the thermals.

Keith took my hand. "If you don't like it, Carole, we'll sell the land and build somewhere else." He'd purchased this land of his dreams in early 2001, five months before Gretchen died. His dream then her resting place, and he was willing to give it up for me.

My heart soared and my breathing eased. "This is the most beautiful place I've ever seen."

We climbed to the next plateau and followed the ridgeline. Sunlight dappled the forest floor in shades of brown, yellow, and green. At the top, a grand oak straddled the mountain's slopes, both dark and light. Gretchen's tree. "She told me and many of her friends she wanted to visit this place," Keith said. She never did. So here among the dry oak leaves Keith and Alex had scattered her ashes.

Arms wide, I hugged the coarse bark of Gretchen's tree, and Keith did the same on the other side, but the trunk was too large for our hands to reach. "I think Gretchen was like that," he said. "You want to wrap your arms around her but can't quite do it."

To comfort him, I shifted right, pressing my cheek into the bark, and stretched until my fingers touched Keith's hand. In truth, I could not imagine the grief he must have felt, nor did I want to touch that knowing. If I got too close to the loss of his daughter, I'd remember how close I came to losing mine.

We planted the narcissus around the base of Gretchen's tree in recognition that she would always be with us. "It's too late for them to bloom this spring," I said. "But planting the bulbs now rather than on her birthday in the fall will give them a chance to root and bloom next year." After covering the area with forest mulch, we headed back down the mountain.

I slid Gretchen's journal onto the den counter beside the piles of books I planned to read. That wasn't so bad, I thought, not too dangerous. Maybe I am trustworthy. Part of me knew I'd skirted the heart of the issue; the other part patted myself on the back. After all, good choices had brought me to this place, challenging but not frightening, comforting in most ways, where God wanted me to be.

Opening the palms of my hands, I prayed. *I'm grateful for your guidance, but what do you want me to do with the rest of my life?* Perhaps if I took the metaphorical view on personal housebuilding, I'd get an answer. Or maybe I should stop worrying and get on with what needed to be done. Only much later would I figure out why I busied myself with the what, where, when, and how of doing while avoiding the question about who God wanted me to be.

HOUSE SITE

Heathcliff muzzled my hand. It was time for his afternoon walk and "hurry-up," our term for him to relieve himself.

"Go for a walk?" I asked. His ears perked. When I stood, he jumped toward me. I rolled my body away and said, "Off," mimicking the Alexandria shelter's Charm School instructors. Then I faced him again. "Sit." I used the 'up' hand signal. Heathcliff's bottom brushed the floor long enough for me to leash him. "Good boy, Heathcliff, good boy."

I grabbed the treat pouch, pocketed house keys and poop bags, and opened the front door. Heathcliff rushed outside with me in tow. "Practice," I sighed, yanking his leash.

We followed the sidewalk around the townhouse neighborhood, Heathcliff sniffing and marking where other dogs had gone before. Slowly, the din of air, rail, and street traffic gave way to an inner calm, as if I was standing on that first shelf of land at our house site. Again, I sensed the Spirit's mysterious inaudible-audible voice, an answer to my what-now question.

Wait.

Chapter 4

Design

As Heathcliff and I often did on our late afternoon walks, we met José and his fuzzy white Bichon Frise, approaching from the opposite direction. Heathcliff positioned his body in front of me even though there wasn't any danger, except for his own strength and exuberance. I cinched my hand up his leash and tightened my grip to prevent him from lunging ahead and pulling me down but did not correct his instinct to guard. Being protected felt like a novel experience to me, one I rather enjoyed.

"Look, Princess," José said, "it's Heathcliff." Princess yapped and ran the length of her leash toward Heathcliff. We owners chatted while our dogs affirmed each other's scents, a peculiar sight given the size difference. With his chin flat on the ground, Heathcliff's head was as high as Princess standing tall. Because he kept his rump in the air, Princess had to jump on her hind legs to catch his scent. I chuckled as the dogs circled and whirled like a two-horse carousel.

In this large, diverse, bedroom community of townhome owners and renters, people didn't tend to know one another unless they had children or dogs. Since Keith and I no longer had children living with us, we were known by the kids on the playground as "Heathcliff's owners." Our townhouse overlooked the playground, so we heard occasional bad language spoken by some of the kids, most from the neighborhood, a few from outside. Keith had told me he once ran off a drug dealer. Even so, walking the neighborhood with Heathcliff felt safe, day or night. Pole lights with light-sensors in front of every townhouse and well-placed streetlights illuminated sidewalks and parking lots. And Heathcliff's deep hackles-up growl gave fair warning to strangers.

After Princess and Heathcliff finished their height-challenged greeting, José and I wished each other a good evening. As Heathcliff and I walked along, he sniffed, marked, and watched for dangers. The first night he'd spent with us, he curled in his bed on the floor beside ours then moved to the top of the stairs in view of our bedroom and the front door. Guarding was part of his nature. When I visited my mother in Connecticut, Heathcliff would not settle unless I opened my bedroom door so he could guard her door, too.

He had not done well in the shelter, the staff said, due to stress from being penned up and surrounded by near constant barking. They were glad to find a home for this big, untrained guy. Heathcliff wanted to obey the rules, but movement, sound, and scents distracted him—behavior I indulged to feed his curiosity or corrected to reinforce his training. A winsome dog, he paused to smell sweet-scented roses, lilies, and peonies during our walks. Less welcome surprises also stopped him in his tracks. Cardboard boxes where they weren't supposed to be, jack-o-lanterns, ghosts or other Halloween decorations, and two-eyed snowmen caused him to shy, cower, and growl. He approached with caution, circled wide, then huddled next to me. I rather enjoyed protecting him, since that seemed natural to me. A squirrel scampered up the maple tree several yards ahead of us, and I jerked Heathcliff's leash to remind him of his training.

Keith and I had adopted eight-month-old Heathcliff after I sold my house in Baltimore and moved to Keith's newly renovated townhouse in Alexandria two years ago. Since we were too old to have children together, we'd decided to adopt a dog, not as a child substitute but to grow our relationship. As with housebuilding, giving a shelter dog a home became a shared mission, a calling we were meant to do. For the next two years, I commuted, and Keith managed dog training, which suited me since I found disciplining Heathcliff difficult. I'd had similar challenges as a parent. I wasn't permissive, just impatient, and inconsistent. Even though I knew inconsistency would confuse Heathcliff—and compromise my partnership with Keith—when pressed by other things on my checklist, I put Heathcliff's bowl on the floor without waiting for him to sit. Why was he so stubborn? Why couldn't he behave without constant reinforcement? Why couldn't he grow up? I'd asked similar questions of my daughter while I raised her. Why was she so stubborn? Why couldn't she behave? But my last question I directed toward myself.

As Heathcliff and I crossed the street at the end of the townhouse development and headed home, I narrowed my eyes and gazed into the unfocused distance. Why can't I grow up and behave like an adult? Why do I get so angry when the world doesn't go the way I want it to? Why do I give in? Now this: why can't I "leave it" and drop the past in the palm of God's hand?

Taking over Heathcliff's care during my sabbatical gave me an opportunity to explore those questions while stepping up to the responsibility. Since I didn't have much co-parenting experience, having raised my children by myself from their grade-school years on, I played to my strength. Every day, I designed Heathcliff's training program like mental lesson plans consistent with his Charm School instruction. Behavioral objectives: Heathcliff will be able to sit, lie down, stay, come, hurry-up, and calmly socialize with people and other dogs. At the end of the day, I evaluated our progress. The objectives-design-implement-evaluate process reminded me of how Keith and I approached marriage—and house-building. As building plans moved toward implementation, we adjusted the original design, accommodating chimneys, woodstoves, ductwork, electric and plumbing, roof insulation to code, and extra beams to support the height. Then we assessed the results vis-à-vis our objectives together, as a couple.

Before calling it a day, Heathcliff and I entered the playground's fenced dog run for some off leash play time. He caught his frisbee when I threw it but wouldn't bring it back to me, or if he did, wouldn't "leave it" when I held out my hand. To him, teasing was part of the game. To me, following the rules was more important—and I don't like to be teased. He soon dropped the frisbee at the far end of the dog run and wandered around sniffing.

When a blond lab mix named Buddy and his owner showed up, I breathed a sigh of relief. Heathcliff would get the exercise he needed. Buddy and Heathcliff romped in the open playing field, chasing old tennis balls, tussling over the frisbee, and tumbling into mouthing and play-biting. They took turns being the top dog while the other bellied-up.

All too soon, Buddy and his owner had to go home. "Heathcliff, come," I called. He loped in my direction, snorting, panting, and grinning his pleasure. While fastening Heathcliff's leash, I noticed a young woman sitting on the playground bench near the swings and holding a Chihuahua to her chest. As we drew near, Heathcliff hopped, glanced at me, and whined.

"He wants to visit your dog," I said. "He's big but gentle." She must have trusted my words or Heathcliff's behavior and her dog's because she stooped and placed the little dog on the grass at her feet. The Chihuahua shivered but held its ground as my big guy approached. A few inches away from the Chihuahua, Heathcliff folded his legs like a sphinx, bellied down, and leaned forward, nose-to-nose with his new friend.

I relaxed my grip on his leash. Though distractible and stubborn, Heathcliff didn't have a mean bone in his body.

Unlike the not-very-grown-up me. There was no protection from her anger.

Chapter 5

Financing

It was mid-September, and we had not secured financing for our mountain house. One morning, an extended telephone conversation with the construction loan officer in charge of our application ended in a deal-breaking impasse. I hung up the phone and closed the spreadsheet in disgust. Praying for help never occurred to me. To my thinking, this was my job.

Since there was nothing to be done about house financing until Keith got home from work, I moved to the next item on my checklist: Gretchen's journal. I came upon this entry, written during her sophomore year.

> **October 11, 1996**: "I was angry today. I am still, but my cursed dual manner of thinking has taken over again and it's as poisonous as before. As I was leaving German class with bitterness because I have problems concentrating, I thought of how pointless it was, to not be able to control your mind no matter how you'd like to. My brain seems like it's on crack, I can't look at anything and comprehend it."

Coincidence? The entry's words fueled my frustration: angry, poisonous thoughts, bitterness about not being able to control the situation no matter how hard I tried, my brain hijacked and unable to comprehend anything. Pointless. Everything I'd done was pointless. I abandoned her journal and chose a book from the top of my fiction pile, hoping to accomplish something, anything to salvage the day. But I was too upset to concentrate. As a last resort, I gave the townhouse a punishing cleaning.

Later, after walking and feeding Heathcliff, I sat in the den, waiting for Keith. My fingers drummed the table, pinky to index. Though our builder had installed the joists to support the main floor, we didn't have enough cash to pay him and his crew.

"How'd it go today?" Keith called as he walked through the front door and into the den. "Any news from the bank?" This was the moment I'd waited for all day.

I took a deep breath, crossed my arms tight over my chest, and let loose. "I faxed every single page of our investment, retirement, and insurance policies to the construction loan guy in Utah. Every. Single. Page." I counted the words on my fingers. "Then I went over everything with him for at least an hour on the phone. The conventional loan people in the Florida branch want copies of everything, too. And some of our documentation is getting lost between Utah and Florida. Every single day, I answer the same questions and respond to more requests for duplicate documentation. Every. Single. Day." Three words, three fingers, pointing at Keith.

He stopped in front of me and stiffened. "Are you done?"

"No." I dropped my chin. Eagerness to share bad news was hardly a welcome after his long day at work. "There's something important we need to discuss."

"Tell me at dinner. I'm going upstairs to change clothes."

A burst of heat jolted my body. Stung by his dismissal—and furious with myself—I stomped into the kitchen. I opened the refrigerator and grabbed broccoli crowns, cremini mushrooms, and chicken breasts, slapping them onto the counter. Heathcliff's nose tracked every movement.

"Go to your bed." I snapped my fingers and pointed to the den. Ears back, he slunk away and lay down on the carpet in the living room. I didn't bother to correct him. While pounding the chicken breasts with a tenderizing mallet, I glanced over the bar counter and saw Heathcliff sitting up, his head cocked like the RCA Victor dog. At least he doesn't hold a grudge, I thought, always hopeful, always optimistic, always forgiving. Why can't I be like that? Because you don't want to, I answered myself. Besides, my anger is perfectly justified. Right?

The aroma rising from the frypan cooled the steam pouring out of my body. After carrying serving dishes to the table, Keith lit the candles, filled our wine glasses, and said grace. Humbled by his prayer of thanksgiving, I waited until we served ourselves before delivering my speech.

"The bank wants copies of the trusts we set up with our lawyers—every single page, including medical directives."

I glared into Keith's intense blue eyes. His shock of white hair, wrestler's shoulders, and rugged face gave him the look of a seasoned pugilist. The guy I counted on to have my back.

"That's ridiculous." He cut a piece of chicken Marsala. "Most of what's in our trusts has nothing to do with money. It's none of their business. They only need to know we have resources."

I cocked my head. "What if we offer to send copies of all the pages with information relating to our finances and nothing else?"

"That's reasonable. If our refusal to share private information means no construction loan, then so be it." I nodded. "Don't worry, Carole, we'll get the house built. It might take a bit longer, that's all. Good dinner, Sweetheart, thank you."

Candlelight flickered in Keith's eyes as he smiled at me. I inhaled his optimism and tasted hope. My shoulders relaxed. Reaching across the table, I took his open hand, as he had taken mine the first night we met.

We spoke about the poured foundation and other construction details inspected during our Labor Day weekend site-visit with the builder. In the living room, Heathcliff's moans escalated into loud whines. He wanted to lick our plates. Now.

"Be quiet, Heathcliff." I used my stern teacher's voice. "Wait." He exhaled a long sigh of discontent. Our adolescent. Keith chuckled softly, and I grinned.

As soon as Keith picked up our dinner plates, Heathcliff bounded into the kitchen. "Wait," Keith said. Heathcliff struggled to remain in his "sit" and keep his nose up as Keith placed the plates on the floor. "Okay." Heathcliff dove for the plates and licked them clean.

The next morning, while walking Heathcliff, I examined my behavior from the previous day. Why all the Sturm und Drang? Of course, I knew why. I'd done everything in my power to succeed and feared my effort might not be enough. I'd quit my job to be with Keith and oversee the building of our house, and I was failing on both counts, as a housebuilder and a wife. And whenever failure dogged my steps, I spewed self-righteous blame in self-defense or wallowed in the Land of Self-Pity. I complained, preferably during dinner because of the captive audience.

How strange. I like to complain. Where did that come from?

I reached into memory and found the answer. When I was in grade school, each member of my family spoke at the dinner table one at a time for two minutes. No, it was two minutes to complain. Ritualized complaining. My family's ritual hadn't seemed strange to me at the time—I thought complaining was normal and everyone behaved that way. But I'd also believed we were superior to other families, perfect in many ways, and happy. Now, memories of our complaining made me uncomfortable, because the adult me knew complaining indicated imperfection, a character flaw, and unhappiness. Maybe we weren't who I thought we were. Maybe something was wrong with my family.

At dinner, my father presided from the captain's chair at the head of the dining room table. After serving us and passing our plates, he unbuckled his wristwatch, placed it on the table, and waited for the second hand to hit twelve. Then he pointed to Mother—she always went first.

"Go," he said.

Mother put down her fork and said something like this: "I did eleven loads of laundry this week and packed fifteen lunches, eleven and fifteen. Do you realize that's fifty loads and sixty lunches a month and over five hundred a year? And that doesn't include five hours of ironing every week plus sewing, cleaning, grocery shopping, breakfast, and dinner." She counted the tasks on her fingers. After her finale, "I don't think any of you appreciate what I do around here," Mother picked up her fork and speared whatever was on her plate.

While my sisters talked, I wrote a mental script to make sure my woes sounded far worse than theirs. And when it was my turn, I talked as fast as I could.

"Bobby threw rocks while we waited for the bus. He said he was trying to hit the telephone pole. I know he was lying. He was aiming at us. And at recess, I didn't get my turn to swing on the swings. Everybody took longer than allowed and nobody made them get off. Then when we lined up to go back inside, somebody pushed me and I almost fell."

"One minute." Daddy called from the head of the table.

"During snack time, my milk carton spilled. I cleaned it up, and the cafeteria ladies gave me another. The milk was sour, and nobody even cared."

"Thirty seconds."

"The teacher gave us really hard spelling words, and math was boring—just arithmetic tables to memorize."

"Ten seconds."

"And I didn't get to sit with my friends on the way home on the bus." I finished in a rush.

"Time." Daddy picked up his watch, buckled it on his wrist, and held the floor for the rest of dinner. Father Abraham, my sisters and I called him in a teasing, loving way, the shining star in our family. How the child adored her father. How the adolescent struggled to find her own little star separate from the brightness of his. Now, I, the adult wondered how patient my tender-hearted father must have been, a lone male among four complaining females.

Our two-minute complaining sessions ended after younger sister Leslie started school and Mother went back to work. Now we all had important things to talk about at the dinner table. Father Abraham didn't time us anymore, though he often held the floor. He lectured on a variety of topics and sketched everything from telephone poles to human genitalia on the blackboard, which hung on the wall behind his chair in the dining room. I listened carefully.

Ritualized complaining moved to afterschool. Mother made herself a cup of decaf laced with milk, and my sisters and I poured ourselves Cokes. Then we sat around the dining room table while Mother listened to our woes. I told her about my teachers' impossible expectations, friends who might not be friends anymore, and all the terrible things that happened that day. At the end of my recital, I got up from the table, feeling much better, and started my homework.

Other times, when I felt down and wandered the house, I'd talk to Mother alone at the kitchen table. "You're very attractive, Carole," she'd say to comfort me. That's nice, I'd think, but that's not what I want. My older sister Jane was the smart one bound for a career, my parents said. I was the pretty one who would marry. Our younger sister Leslie was Leslie, a smart beauty with racehorse legs and big brown eyes like our father. I wanted it all.

When Mother had a bad day, one of us would be the listener at the kitchen table. We compared notes later. Mother would fold her hands and say, "You see, my father never liked me. I was always to blame, like Eve in the Bible. Nobody understood me." To avoid provoking her pound-the-table anger by saying something that might have been perceived as disagreement, I didn't say anything. But I listened carefully.

Then she'd say, "You know, your father thinks women aren't as smart as men."

Our Father Abraham? Could that be true? I never asked.

After feeding Heathcliff his breakfast, I poured a cup of coffee laced with milk then emailed our decision to the construction loan officer. While waiting for a response, I busied myself with chores and thought about my family. Why didn't I tell Mother what I was thinking or ask about what she said about my father? I thought we talked about everything.

By late morning, I still hadn't heard from the loan officer. I fumed. Why are hope and optimism so hard for me? And why do I struggle with trust—trusting people when I shouldn't and not trusting God when I should? More questions without answers. To pass the time, I read Gretchen's short story "Rain" before breaking for lunch.

The story, based on her own experience recorded in her journal, was about how young love evolved into lasting friendship. At the end, she wrote, "Angels dance in the sky, God wills their wings to vanish, and they fall gently, like parachutes, to every corner of the earth." The fallen angels she referenced were herself and her trusted friend Paul, a man whose name was on Keith's—now our—Christmas card list.

"He's a good quality guy," Keith had told me more than once. On another occasion, when I waited for more, he added pensively, "I would have loved any man for loving and caring for my daughter."

I sat in the den, pondering my questions and Gretchen's words. A partial answer formed in my mind. I don't trust God because I, too, am a fallen angel who wants to make her world the way it was before the fall. Perfect. But whatever I do, it's never enough because the world is still a chaotic mess. And failure to live up to expectations brings out the beast in me. The beast who rejects God's grace as my family did. The beast who feeds on fear.

The beast who is the angry, not-very-grown-up me I hide behind a wall of complaints.

Chapter 6

The Basement

After all my fussing, we received approval for our construction loan in early October. We still had to qualify for rollover from construction to conventional loan—more part-time work for me. Though we'd cut it close, everything associated with our housebuilding, from the basement up, was moving forward on schedule, as if it was meant to be.

One Saturday, Keith and I made the three-hour drive to the mountain to check the progress. While I navigated Route 29 south, Heathcliff painted the back windows of the car with nose prints then propped his big head on Keith's broad shoulder and sniffed. On the floor at Keith's feet, asleep in her glass terrarium, lay Gretchen's childhood turtle, Penny.

"Have I told you about the day I gave Penny to Gretchen?" Keith asked.

"Yes, but tell me again." Keith's stories often gained detail and nuance in the retelling, as if he was both reliving the past and probing its meaning—as I was.

Keith cleared his throat. "It was soon after Gretchen was crawling. She was a rambunctious child and rough on things when she got excited. So, I thought a turtle might be a good first pet, an eastern box turtle I named Penelope, Penny for short."

I glanced down at Penny's high domed carapace, brown and patterned like a quilt with yellow rectangles and streaks. Her brown eyes were ringed with gold, and her claws were long, slender, and straight. Her upper jaw featured the distinct beak of a box turtle. At the time Keith brought her home, she already possessed the ability to protect herself from harm: her shell's open plastron could hinge shut, enclosing her body in a hard shell.

"When Gretchen spotted me holding the turtle, she scooted across the kitchen floor. I washed Penny with soap in the kitchen sink, clearing bacteria, and placed her on the floor."

"Gretchen liked her turtle?"

"In her own way. First, she studied the turtle. Then she rocked and lunged after Penny, gurgling and shouting. Whenever Gretchen got too close, Penny pulled into her shell. When Gretchen moved away, Penny hinged open and resumed walking, with Gretchen in eager pursuit." Keith drank from his thermal travel mug and gazed out the window, perhaps savoring both coffee and memories.

"What was she like as a toddler?"

"Gretchen was curious about everything. Whenever I was going somewhere, she always wanted to come. Always." He turned to look at Heathcliff, perched in the back of the Subaru and taking in the three-sided panorama. Guarding.

"I kept a vegetable garden in those early years. Gretchen would follow me into the garden, taking one bite out of each tomato and leaving them on the vine."

I burst out laughing. I hadn't heard this story before.

"When I discovered what she'd done, I didn't scold her. I'd told her they were for eating, and she was only pursuing her curiosity. Instead, I explained that tomatoes were for everyone's enjoyment when they were red and fully-grown."

"And..." I chuckled.

"Gretchen said, 'Okay, I understand,' and stopped biting the tomatoes too early."

While Keith lapsed into his thoughts, another often-told story replayed in my head.

Keith was picking up his children for the weekend soon after the divorce, and his ex-wife told him she was worried. Six-year-old Gretchen had been pulling wings and legs off insects—spiders, dragonflies, and grasshoppers—popping bees with matches, and scorching beetles using the sun through a magnifying lens. Aware of the psychological implications of this behavior, Keith sat down with her on the front door stoop when they arrived at his house.

"Why are you hurting small creatures, Gretchen?" he asked.

"I don't know, I guess they're scary and sneaky, so I don't like them."

"They are little, Gretchen, and they have their own little lives and families. They have things they need to do to live. To them, you are a big scary giant who catches them and pulls off their legs and laughs. That's much scarier. They try to protect themselves by biting or stinging you or by rushing away. But they are really just fuzzy little guys with lots of extra legs and eyes."

Her chin dropped to her chest. She wiped her cheek with her wrist and nodded. "Okay, I understand."

I glanced at Keith. "Gretchen's response to your correction about biting the tomatoes was the same as with the small creatures."

He nodded. "I had no idea how well that lesson would take. From then on, Gretchen loved rescuing small creatures. Her friends and co-workers at her memorial told many stories of Gretchen harboring snakes, frogs, toads, and turtles, shooing or carrying them off the road. She saved bees wounded by jump ropes, worms drowning after a heavy rain, and many others."

I felt the sting of guilt. I, too, had cared for small creatures, except for one. *Later*, the Spirit said, *even if you've told him already, tell him again, the real story, no secrets.*

As we drove up the old logging road that led to our land, my thoughts returned to Gretchen and her turtle. "Did she take Penny with her after the divorce?"

"No, Penny stayed with me. Gretchen took care of her when she visited every other weekend, and I fed Penny between visits. When Gretchen and Alex moved in with me, she took over Penny's care. She had another turtle in college—Penny stayed with me then, too." And after Gretchen's death. I felt the weight of Keith's words. Penny had stayed with him for thirty-three years. Now we were letting her go.

I parked in the shade of the driveway pullout below the mountain house and grabbed my jacket. Keith opened the back hatch for Heathcliff. Walking through the framed basement, we noted garage, utility and laundry rooms, the man cave, and stairwell areas. I took pictures, including one of Heathcliff, peering out the back door of the dark man cave. Then we climbed the slope to the main level and studied the newly installed radiant floor warm boards.

After our inspection, we retrieved Penny from the car and carried her down the driveway to the large turn-around on our property at the end of the mountain road. Heathcliff raced ahead, running into the woods and up the mountainside. The hinge of Penny's plastron remained shut.

"Should we mark the edge of Penny's shell?" I asked. "That way, whenever we see a box turtle, we can tell whether or not it's Penny."

"No, she needs to go on with her turtle life as is. And this way we'll think we're seeing her everywhere." He placed her beside the mossy stream that flows down a ravine from the ridge above the house site, the ridge where Gretchen's tree grows. "There'll be lots of grubs and worms for her to eat here."

Penny's stubby legs and long-necked head emerged, her upper jaw displaying the distinct beak. Like some primordial creature, she reared up on her front legs, extended her head, and craned her neck like the letter J. Her gold-ringed, brown eyes surveyed her new territory. Then, after three decades in captivity, Penny marched into her natural habitat.

I stared at the spot where Penny had disappeared beneath the moss and leaf litter. Part of me felt relieved, unburdened, happy to "leave it," and distance myself from the past. Another part wanted to reach out and pull her back, to hold onto Gretchen's childhood pet, protect her, and keep her safe. I balled my hands and girded my body, resisting the temptation.

Gentle breezes, drifting down the ravine, rustled leaves and caressed our faces. The sun shone through the topmost tree branches and backlit the autumn leaves, creating a surround of yellow and gold like clerestory windows set with stained glass. I sensed we were standing in a roofless cathedral, a bowered sanctuary.

I lifted my eyes to the ridgeline. "Do you think Gretchen's ashes are still on the mountain after almost a decade?"

"Some might have mixed with the soil. Most likely they blew into the air. In any given breath, we could be inhaling her molecules, anyone's molecules, even Galileo's."

The treetops swayed, whirling, and I with them, almost losing my balance. To steady myself, I planted my feet and stared at the cathedral's earthen floor. God formed us from clay, the dust of the earth. In the end, we are but dust. I breathed in deeply and held the molecules in my lungs for as long as I could. Then I let them go.

"Heathcliff, come," I called. He bounded down the ridge and out of the woods then followed us up the driveway to the car.

On the drive home, Keith gazed out the passenger side window again while Heathcliff kept his back-of-the-car vigil. I imagined Gretchen, talking to lizards, toads, and turtles—as I had at her age and still did—

the voice of a child who could have been mine. The closeness I felt at the mountain returned, along with thoughts about the kind of house we were building.

Stop running and tell him, the Spirit said, *even though the truth is uncomfortable.* The truth hidden away in my mind's dark basement.

My eyebrows rose, tensing my forehead. "I don't remember if I've mentioned this before, but when I was Gretchen's age, I had an encounter with a small creature. But I learned a different lesson." My voice quavered.

"Yes…"

Would he think less of me if I told him the real truth? Surely, he'd understand, having gone through this with Gretchen. Except I'd discovered something terrible about myself that day. And, unlike Gretchen's story, there was no redemption and no freedom from guilt.

Tell him. Now. Go into the heart of danger.

I made a conscious effort to lower my eyebrows. Then I took a deep breath and told the story, the images ever vivid in my child's memory.

I was perched on the stone out-cropping in the field in front of our house in Connecticut, reading a Little Golden Book. At the end of the story, I closed the book and rubbed my fingers along the shiny foil spine. A flying grasshopper leaped across my lap into a clump of hay weeds at my feet. She was golden brown, about an inch and a half long, with large eyes, two antennae, two pairs of wings, and long hind legs.

Though the grasshopper was eating, I wanted to catch her and study her up close. I tucked the book under my arm and cupped my hands. She jumped and flew out of reach. I chased her around the field. Each time I stooped and reached, she got away. My gut churned red-hot. I followed the sneaky grasshopper across the driveway and onto the paved turnaround where she landed. Without thinking, I crouched, grabbed the book with both hands, and slammed it down.

The slap echoed in my brain. I sat back on my haunches, slack-jawed, limbs numb. The enormity of my crime crept into consciousness. I'd never killed anything before. Staring at the Little Golden Book, I imagined slimy green, yellow, and brown guts smeared across the front cover. Blood rushed back into my body. I quickly hid my hands behind my back. Then I stood, backed up, and slipped away, leaving the book on the driveway. If I didn't see the book, maybe I wouldn't think about the grasshopper, and nobody would know.

THE BASEMENT

Late that afternoon, my family climbed into our black '49 Chevrolet and headed out for hamburger specials at the local truckers' joint on Route 8 north of Seymour. As Daddy backed the car into the turnaround, my older sister Jane pointed out the book I'd left on the driveway.

"Carole," Mother scolded, "pick up the book when we get back. We can't have things like that left around. You must learn to pick up your things."

My father added in his deep, stern voice, "We can't afford to leave good things outside. Pick up the book as soon as we get back."

When we got home at dusk, I offered to take my bath first, hoping everyone had forgotten about the Little Golden Book. I climbed into the tub just before Mother stomped into the bathroom. "Carole. Your father told me you didn't pick up your book."

"I'm sorry." I took a deep breath and wailed. "There's a squashed grasshopper underneath the book! I killed her! I killed her!" My body could be cleansed, but guilt soiled my heart and soul.

Later, Daddy came to tuck me into bed. "Carole, there wasn't anything under the book." The tension in my shoulders dissolved, and my head sank deep into the pillow.

"I am not a killer," I whispered over and over after he left.

"I am not a killer. I am not a killer."

I stared at the road ahead, fearing the disapproval that might be on Keith's face. Then I scowled. No more hiding the truth or excusing my offense. My voice hardened. "Of course, I was guilty. I meant to kill that grasshopper."

"Why didn't your father teach you the lesson I taught Gretchen? I always told my children the truth."

"I don't know." I was surprised by the gentle delivery of his question, having expected a rebuke. "My parents always told us the truth, at least I thought they did." I chewed my lip. "There's something about that story I've never figured out. I even wrote about the grasshopper for a creative writing class during freshman year in college." I'd found the draft titled, "To Kill," in my closet. An unresolved memory, hidden but not forgotten.

I resisted an urge to bite my nails, all ten of them, one hand after the other. "My question is, why does that silly story still haunt me?" Why couldn't I "leave it"?

Chapter 7

House Framing

A week after our trip to the mountain, I drove to Connecticut with Heathcliff. In Seymour, we exited Route 8, passed the Dairy Queen, and turned toward Woodbridge. Minutes later, I veered left onto Sanford Road and drove the half-mile to the stop sign at Newton. The old neighborhood, Round Hill, the foundation and frame of my youth. Since there were no other vehicles around, I rolled the windows down and let the car idle. Perhaps because I'd been learning about Gretchen's childhood, I decided to revisit mine with more discerning eyes.

Ahead was the spring-fed pool my father had built for the Russells, owners of Round Hill Farm, a year before I was born. Now a locked fence and overgrown shrubbery surrounded the pool, which hadn't been drained and cleaned in years. To the left above the expanse of lawn—the scene of the many neighborhood picnics Mother had organized—stood the Russells' saltbox house, dating from the eighteenth century. Beyond the Big Maple, which I alone had summited, had been the barn apartment above the farm office where my family lived while Daddy completed his medical studies. I could almost smell the wild pink roses, which blossomed below the ramp to the second-floor apartment on Father's Day.

During the post-war years, housing had been in short supply, and money was something made of nothing. Jane and I jumped on our lumpy mattresses, rode tricycles around the living room, and snuck down the back stairs to spy on Howie, the farm's hired hand. Young and deeply tanned, Howie blew cigarette smoke out of his nose and sang "Big Rock Candy Mountain" while painting the barns and houses on the Russell property. Like Daddy, Howie always grinned when we talked with him while he worked. "Yup, uh-huh, is that so," he'd say.

Still idling at the intersection, I gazed right, up the gentle hill to our next home, the house where Mother still lived. After Leslie's birth, my family had rented the three-bedroom, one-bathroom ranch. To have a spare room, we three girls slept in one bedroom with beds lined up like piano keys. Jane and I continued our companionable adventures until one day I decided to take all the toys out of the homemade plywood toybox, which was placed in the corner of the dining room below the blackboard. Colored blocks, a slunk-out slinky, pull trains, and unstacked cups scattered across the floor.

"Don't touch the toys." Jane's red hair flashed as she grabbed each toy and placed it correctly back in the toybox. "Not that one, and not that one either, no, no, no." With my eyes fixed on Jane, I reached my hand toward the toybox just to see if I could provoke her. "The toys are mine," she yelled. "Don't. Touch. Any. of them." But I wanted to. Mother looked up from her ironing in the kitchen. I wanted her attention, too, preferably at Jane's expense.

I rolled up the front windows and shook my head. Why that memory now? The past is past, isn't it? Heathcliff whined in anticipation. Turning right onto Newton, I glimpsed other houses through the trees. I didn't know many of the neighbors anymore. Neither did Mother. I took a sharp left, drove up the driveway, parked in the turnaround, and let Heathcliff out. He raced across the lawn, scenting, marking, and chewing sticks that had fallen since our last visit.

Mother didn't meet us at the door. I figured she was napping in her chair and didn't hear our arrival. So, I pushed the button hidden under the secret shingle to open the garage door and called to Heathcliff. Into the garage and through the door to the breezeway, he loped. I retrieved the hidey key from a hook in the furnace room and glanced up at the small scatter-shot hole in the corner of the breezeway ceiling. Fifty-three years ago, a man came to rob our house, and he hurt my mother. "The accident." The simple version, the child's version, which was all my sisters and I knew.

I dropped my purse in the kitchen and headed to the living room. Mother opened her eyes when we entered the room. "Oh, there you are," she said. I kissed her, and Heathcliff did his usual snort-and-grin greeting then perched his hip on her chair's footrest, hoping for a rump rub.

Mother chuckled and reached for her cane to use as a back scratcher. "What a good dog."

"I'm going to hit the bathroom then make some tea. Would you like a cup of decaf?"

"That would be lovely."

A few minutes later, I returned with hot mugs and, after clearing mail-order packages off the living room sofa, sat down. Mother and I caught up with the news—the weather, Jessica, David, Keith, house-framing. I slipped off my shoes, curled my legs onto the sofa, and cupped my hands around the warm mug. Our conversation lapsed into comfortable silence. The mantle clock ticked, and the old hot-water radiators snapped. Sprawled at Mother's feet, Heathcliff's body quivered. His legs twitched, and he growled, chasing critters in his dream.

Out of nowhere, Mother said, "When people ask about my limp and I tell them, some say, 'Oh, but if I had been there, that would never have happened to me. I would have stopped him.'" She harrumphed. "I think to myself, wait till you've looked down the barrel of a shotgun. But I don't say anything."

The event that marked my family's before and after, the event that framed my youth, the past that would never be past. I placed my strong right foot on the floor and shifted my weight as I leaned toward her. "What made you think about that now, Mother?"

"I guess these days I have a lot of time to sit in my chair and think."

Maybe this was an opening. "I was so young when it happened. I don't remember much."

"Oh..." Mother's voice sounded like a frightened child.

My weak left foot dropped to the floor, and my jaw clamped shut. Heathcliff must have heard Mother's small cry or seen her body shrink or smelled her anguish, because he got up, walked around her chair, and put his big head on her shoulder. Guarding.

Don't upset your mother, I heard in my head. Don't worry your mother.

For as long as I can remember, Mother's anxiety was something my family tried to make into nothing. She took medication and did her best to hide her distress, and we did our best to avoid doing or saying anything that would upset her. When overwhelmed, Mother's anxiety often took the form of steam-coming-out-of-her-ears, table-pounding anger, which I could deal with if I kept my head about me and my mouth shut. But anything having to do with "the accident" made me want to protect her like Heathcliff did—and honor our family's unspoken agreement not to talk about it. For if we talked about "the accident," we'd have to acknowledge our home as a crime scene and what happened there as beyond our control.

Even though I wanted to know the truth, Mother's anxiety put me on high alert. Hair rose on the back of my neck. Air sucked out of my lungs. Blood pulsed in my veins. I had made a mistake. By venturing into the heart of danger, I'd taken Mother there, too. My chin dropped to my chest, and my mind narrowed then played a scene from forty years ago.

I stood in the front yard, jangling car keys, on my way to see my high school boyfriend one last time before leaving for college. Mother hung out the breezeway door. "Don't rebel, don't rebel," she said. Though I heard her screech, the thought that she feared what I, the pretty one who would marry, might be doing with him never occurred to me. Glancing above Mother's shoulder, I saw the small scatter-shot hole in the corner of the breezeway ceiling. In my head, her words morphed into a plea: "Don't leave me, please, don't leave me." I thought: Don't worry, Mother, I won't—even though I knew I would. Someday, I'd have to leave home. Someday.

Now, forty years later, I stood in the living room of my childhood home, shaking my head again, this time in an attempt to banish the conflation of memory, imagination, and fear. Failing that, I pushed everything aside, as I had Gretchen's journals on first read. Safe distance. Figure it out later. Then I did what I'd always done.

Changed the subject.

"What would you like to watch on TV tonight?" I lowered the living room window shades and switched on the inside lights to protect the person who had protected me—all of us.

"Let me see what's on." Mother picked up the newspaper's TV schedule from the end table next to her chair. "There's *Wheel of Fortune* and *Jeopardy*, then reruns of *Murder, She Wrote*. I do love Angela Lansbury, she's so clever."

"Yes, she always solves the crimes and catches the criminals." Comforting and predictable. I rose from the sofa. "How 'bout I unpack the car, feed Heathcliff, and make us some dinner. We can eat in front of the TV if you'd like."

"That would be lovely." Mother leaned back and pulled a flannel blanket over her face. I suppressed a sigh.

While making dinner, I realized I, too, hid my face under a blanket—a blanket of silence. Because if I didn't talk about fearful things, I could deny them breath and make the past not true. It did not occur to me that this old frame was the exact opposite of the new house being framed on the mountain.

Chapter 8

Under Roof

One cold pre-dawn morning before Thanksgiving, Heathcliff and I walked the neighborhood in Alexandria and came to a dark stretch with several yard lights out. A squirrel leaped from a tree trunk, darted across our path, and skittered into the darkness between two townhouse blocks. Heathcliff bolted, all one-hundred pounds in single-minded pursuit, like a rebellious adolescent.

I dropped his leash. He had pulled me down before, face first on the playground lawn, knocking the wind out of me and almost dislocating my shoulder. This time I chose to release him rather than risk hitting concrete.

"Heathcliff." I loud whispered into the space where I'd last seen him, not wanting to wake anyone. Seconds ticked like minutes. "Heathcliff. Come."

My voice rasped. I imagined him wandering into Franconia Road's traffic, getting struck and killed. Gone. And it was my fault. He was only doing what undisciplined dogs do. Due to my indulgence and inconsistency, I had failed to protect him. Guilty as charged.

I paced the sidewalk. My heart throbbed in my chest and ears. I couldn't change things any more than I could the last time this happened during another dark time in Texas with another adolescent.

I heard the garage door open. *Thank you, God*, I prayed, *she's home.* The time on my clock-radio read 1:37 a.m. I leaped out of bed and flipped on the ceiling lights in the living room.

"You're late again, past curfew." My hands fisted at my side.

Jessica snarled. "So, what? Big deal. You're such a rule follower, Mom."

Any calm I might have had vanished. "Why is it so hard for you to get home on time, Jessica?" I screeched. "You're disrupting the whole household. We need our sleep."

"I can do anything I want."

"Not if you want to live here." I'd drawn the line. The much-avoided line.

"Fine." Jessica strode through the dining room into the kitchen toward the laundry room exit to the garage, car keys in hand.

I went after her. "Leave the keys on the counter."

"What?" She whipped around to face me.

"The car belongs to me." Now I bared my teeth.

Jessica cocked her head then straightened. "Fine." The keys smacked onto the counter. She pushed past me and slammed the front door behind her.

The house trembled. My daughter. Gone.

I stood slump-shouldered in the living room. The ceiling lights illuminated nothing except my failure to stay calm. I didn't know what to do. She'd never run away before, and it was my fault. I had lost control. In truth, I'd never had control.

The throb of my heartbeat broke the audible silence. I paced the living room, dining room, and kitchen, staring out the front window, staring at the kitchen clock, staring at the door, wishing it to open. Window, clock, door. Window, clock, door.

Please God, bring her home, please, please, please, I'll do anything, I'll give up anything, anything you want. I sobbed, prayed, begged, and paced. Kitchen, dining room, living room. Window, clock, door.

Twenty minutes later the front door burst open. Jessica stomped into the living room and stopped several feet in front of me. I released a breath I hadn't known I was holding.

"I'm back." Jessica stood rigid.

"Where did you go, Jessica? I was so worried." I used every bit of my reserve not to pull her into my arms or crumble to the floor.

She hesitated, and I waited. "I walked down Park Road. The police stopped me and asked my name. I told them. Then they said, 'Go home. If you're still here when we make the next round, we'll have to take you in. So, go home, just go home.' So, I did." Her chin dropped. "Because I didn't have any other place to go."

"You will always have a home with me, Jessica." Under my roof. A promise of protection, spoken out of fear and need to rescue. Fear of terrible things that might happen to her. Fear of failing as a parent. Fear of something in plain sight, hiding under a blanket of silence.

Dog tags jangled like car keys, and out of the darkness loped Heathcliff, panting with pleasure, his tongue lolling. As I'd hoped, he returned to the place where he'd left me.

I grabbed his leash. "Don't ever do that again! You scared me to death!"

He snorted and grinned. I knew I should praise him for coming when called and give him a treat to reinforce his training. But I didn't.

"Let's go." I yanked his leash. Heathcliff's ears perked at the word "Go," and we resumed our walk, as dawn's light appeared on the eastern horizon.

That evening, I told Keith about Heathcliff running after the squirrel and my associated memory of Jessica. "Why do I default to anger the moment my fear ends?" I asked. "That's a strange kind of love. Crazy, you know?"

Keith cocked his head. "I got angry with my kids plenty of times, tired and worn out." Me too, me too, I thought, indulging in self-pity. "Gretchen and Alex came to live with me when they were teenagers, and she didn't like to follow the rules either. And she disappeared at night."

He launched into a story about Gretchen, coming home in the wee hours of the morning. "When she unlocked the door and stepped into the front entrance, I asked her where she'd been. 'It's three o'clock,' I said. 'Everyone's been worried.'" Keith pointed to the living room. "We sat down, and I said, 'We care about you, and we've lost a whole night's sleep.' She glared and said, 'Fuck you, Dad. You don't have to worry,' and flipped her hand like she was shooing me away. Then she said, 'And you don't have to love me, I absolve you of that contract.'"

Wide-eyed, I stared at him. "Oh, Keith, what in the world did you say?"

His voice softened. "I told her, 'Love doesn't work that way, Gretchen, especially not the love parents feel for their child.'"

I wondered if his calm had been tempered by time and loss. "And her response?"

"She jumped out of the chair, yelled, 'Go to hell!' and stomped upstairs to her bedroom."

I processed his story for a few moments then asked, "Why did she snap at you?"

Keith sighed. "Gretchen was easy to love and hard to understand. She was polite and good company until people got close. Then she felt vulnerable and cursed to drive people away."

"You, too?"

"Yes, and we talked about that. She knew she couldn't stay with me forever, that she'd have to find someone else to walk through life with. Maybe that's why she pushed me away."

Maybe that's why we must push our parents away in order to leave home, to get out from under their roofs so we can build our own to protect us from the elements, like the mountain house roof now being shingled. Why did the desire to leave home make sense to me as a daughter and teacher but not as a parent? Why did I as a parent morph into the angry beast then remorsefully wimp out and hand my daughter the keys to the car instead of calmly enforcing the rules? Beast and wimp. Why both seemingly opposite weaknesses?

The next morning, while walking Heathcliff and watching for squirrels, I thought about my own adolescence. How I'd gloried in my sexuality, tested my parents' rules, and got grounded for breaking curfew three times in a row. That third night, I found my poor tired Father Abraham waiting as I stepped through the breezeway and unlocked the kitchen door. His deep voice unnerved me. In truth, the confrontation was unpleasant for both of us. There was no discussion the next morning, only the weekend grounding. I never broke curfew again. Perhaps I'd expected the same from Jessica—despite the difference in delivery.

As we approached the townhouse, Heathcliff moaned in hunger, reminding me of the task at hand: breakfast. I descended the basement stairs to the unfinished laundry-storage area, and he raced down after me. After placing his replenished water bowl on the floor, I measured the kibble into his food bowl and held it above his nose.

"Sit." I gave the signal. Heathcliff turned his head and ignored my instructions. I waited. Seconds clicked by as he wandered around the laundry-storage room. All the things I needed to do clamored for attention, but I didn't give in or repeat the instruction.

Heathcliff lowered himself to a sitting position. I gave the "Okay" signal and sighed. Rule-followers might be easier to live with compared to rebellious adolescents. But the love parents feel for their children, both dutiful and prodigal, is not hard to understand.

Chapter 9

Appliances

With the mountain house under roof, Keith and I spent our winter weekends planning the interior. Cabinets, doors, hinges, knobs, or handles—with or without locks—countertops, tile and wood flooring, bathtub, showers, toilets, sinks, faucets, electrical and lighting fixtures, ceiling fans, and appliances. We expected this level of detail and decision-making, having done the same when renovating the townhouse. As with our marriage, we started fresh—different house, different marriage—with the knowledge of what we wanted to do the same and differently. In both cases, I didn't want to make any big mistakes we'd have to live with.

Our builder had an account with Sears, so one evening Keith and I drove to our local store in Landmark Mall to shop for appliances. As we walked the aisles, *Consumer Reports* in hand, and compared styles and brands, I scribbled make and model numbers on a notepad. After we completed our preliminary list, Keith wandered into the electronics department. A glittering array of Home Theaters, LED and Plasma TVs beckoned. While he and an eager salesperson moved from one gleaming big screen to another, I found a place to sit on a low empty shelf. Shopping was like a treasure hunt for Keith. Not for me. If the trip wasn't a quick in-and-out, I soon experienced sensory overload, like "turning up the pressure on a firehose," as Gretchen had described in her journals. Sometimes our connections unsettled me. But I felt comfortable with this one.

Surrounded by TVs and thinking about Gretchen, I remembered what Alex had told me about the ten years they lived with their mother. They ran wild, with no restrictions on TV or play and no set times for sleeping or meals. Every other weekend with Keith, they had rules, bedtimes, and chores. Keith had told me that during weekends with him, they attended church and Sunday school, caught up on doctors' appointments, homework, and projects. Gretchen and Alex learned to cook and eat together, to sit and converse in restaurants without crawling on the floor. They complained about having to stay in their chairs but admitted the food was better at "slow food" restaurants. I'd smiled when hearing that expression, though I knew their childhood years had not been easy. From what Keith had told me, their adolescence was even harder.

Fifteen-year-old Gretchen came to live with Keith at the beginning of her sophomore year of high school—she'd told him that she and her mom were sick of fighting all the time. Alex was thirteen and decided to move in, too. Keith and his newly married wife soon discovered his children were feral, without knowledge of how to manage personal hygiene, clothing, or time. So, Keith and his wife limited phone use and set routines: bedtimes and morning wake up, mealtimes and menus, and chores to keep order in the house. Keith took Gretchen shopping, taught her to pick out and match clothes, and asked a saleslady to fit her with her first bra. Having worked at a shoe store during college, Keith helped Gretchen select heels for her first big dance at school. He assisted with homework and showed his children how to manage their time, select focused topics for long-term projects, and turn their assignments in—on time. Gretchen and Alex improved their grades dramatically. She joined the drama club and literary magazine, contributing both art and writing. And she befriended Rich, a clever, witty, snarky guy Gretchen wrote about in her journals, a fellow much like her, Keith told me.

The morning after we visited Sears, I rummaged around Keith's upstairs file cabinet, looking for owner's manuals for our townhouse appliances to compare them with our mountain house selections. I came upon another Gretchen file folder, one I'd overlooked. Grade-school stories, school pictures, a home-made Father's Day card. Then a white business envelope addressed to Keith with a local psychologist's return address.

I opened the envelope and read.

> **June 1993.** "Gretchen's father found her inside the refrigerator, which concerned him and prompted him to seek treatment for her, revealing new insights. Gretchen said she was just looking for someplace to be alone."

I set the report aside.

When Keith got home and asked me about my day, I handed him the envelope. "I found this in the file cabinet." I felt like an intruder but shielded myself with what he'd said: full access, I could ask him anything.

"Yes." He stood in front of me in the den. Not moving.

"You found her in the refrigerator." I raised my eyebrows.

"No secrets," he said, while adopting a defensive stance. "I thought you knew."

I felt my body soften. How I hated to cause him pain. "What happened?"

We slid into the den chairs, and he told me the story. In the spring of her sophomore year, when Gretchen was sixteen, he came home from work late one afternoon, saw schoolbooks on the dining room table, and sighed. Thinking his children had gone back to their old ways, he called, "Gretchen, Alex, time to start your homework." No answer. He saw Alex sitting outside on the townhouse deck, talking on the phone. Sliding the glass door open, he asked where Gretchen was. "In the house, somewhere," Alex said. Keith called up the stairs to her bedroom. No answer. Then he turned on the basement light and descended the stairs, calling her name. No answer.

I sat stock still, watching Keith relive the scene.

"In the dim beyond the stairwell, I noticed a crack of light peaking from the basement refrigerator. The door was ajar, shelves sitting on the counter. When I opened the refrigerator, Gretchen was tucked above the vegetable bins. Her legs pulled to her chest, head curled under the freezer compartment, and hand gripping the rack on the door. She was a little too big to fit in the space with the door closed. 'What are you doing, Gretchen?' I asked. 'I needed a place to be alone,' she said. I didn't think it was a suicide attempt but immediately made an appointment with the psychologist."

Gretchen's diagnosis: bipolar disorder.

After Keith went upstairs to change into his workout clothes, I thought about how painful it must have been for him, watching this happen to Gretchen. How well I knew. I, too, had sought help for Jessica during difficult times in her adolescence. But when the difficulties happened to me, at the same age as Gretchen, there wasn't any professional help.

I set the psychologist's report aside and rubbed the back of my neck. This connection point was acutely uncomfortable. Maybe if I distanced myself from those fearful times, I could make them not true. But wouldn't withholding the truth of my past from Keith, especially after he'd told me about Gretchen's, be a mistake?

Go into the heart of danger, the Spirit said. *Remember what happened. No secrets.*

Do it, I told myself. Do it.

Tomorrow.

Chapter 10

Paint Colors

The next morning, I emailed the final list of appliances with make and model numbers to our builder. Then I reread the psychologist's report. Gretchen was demonstrating unusual behaviors, the report stated, very socially isolated, very defended against closeness, and not interested in relationships with people.

"In fact, she verbalizes that she sees no point in talking to people," the psychologist wrote. She was also very angry but unable to deal with those feelings. "Gretchen herself has noted that her mood changes quickly and drastically. She is prone to periods of depression. However, she is not interested in taking medication at this time." The report concluded, "...it is critical that she get help now so that hopefully she can develop resources to cope with stressful events in her life..." Anger. Depression. Alone.

After my first husband left, I sought professional help for both my children and me, because I was a stressed-out mess. During the day, I spewed anger and blame about him to anyone who would listen. Then night after night, I crouched in the closet I'd shared with him and muffled cries into a workout shirt pulled from the laundry. The shirt smelled of my own sweat, an appalling odor. For the first time in my life, I truly and thoroughly hated myself.

"How could I have worked so hard and failed so miserably?" I wailed. I felt like I was falling down a deep well, helpless to fight the darkness closing around me. Attempts to grab the slippery, wet, crumbling walls were all futile. My entire reality was a pinhole of light at the top of the well, shrinking to nothing.

One evening, disgusted with all my childish bawling, I wiped my face and dropped the workout shirt into the laundry bin. I'm free to choose,

I thought. No one stands in my way. Why not me? Why not believe in God like my friends and colleagues? I walked out of the dark closet. More accurately, God lifted me out though I'm not sure why, because I was furious.

"Okay, I give up," I said, "I believe in you. Aren't. You. Lucky? Now fix this mess."

God rewarded me with silence. Alone, I survived on three hours of sleep per night at best. My 5-foot-5-body dropped below one hundred pounds. Instead of crying in my closet at night, worries plagued me while I lay in bed. Am I prepared to teach tomorrow's classes? Does Jessica need stitches for her scraped knee? How am I going to pay for David's new glasses?

One night, while running through the next day's worry list, I fell into an exhausted sleep. I woke in the wee hours with my arms reaching straight up as if seeking help while my fingernails raked down one arm after the other after the other. My jaw ached and popped from clenching my teeth. When I got up to do my pre-dawn workout, the sun rose in psychedelic colors—terrifying hallucinations. I knew I had to humble myself or die.

As I sipped my morning coffee, I pondered that scene from twenty years ago and the freedom from fear I craved. Freedom from the same well Gretchen fell into, and I with her upon first reading her journals. Maybe that's why beige is my safe color for decorating, a fallback even though I love to wear clothing in bright jewel tones: sapphire blue, ruby red, amethyst purple, and emerald green. Shades of beige versus jewel colors. A duality. I recalled the passage from Gretchen's journal, "I was angry today... my cursed dual manner of thinking has taken over again and it's as poisonous as before." Something I might have written if I'd kept a journal as a teenager. Not about the angry, blaming, complaining, grasshopper-killing beast, but a demon unchecked and spewing poison. The poisonous demon also rose unbidden for the first time during my junior year of high school.

I was doing homework in my room one night. By then, my parents had purchased the rental house and added a wing of bedrooms, so I was alone. Out of nowhere, a voice shrieked inside my head: "You're a fraud, and you know it. You're not smart. You're stupid, ugly, and fake." Copying vocabulary words was inexplicably difficult. Thought and movement ground to a halt. Unbearable tension crept from my shoulders and neck up the back of my head and into my forehead. Blinding pressure built. I drew the same letters repeatedly, pressing the pencil deeper into a pad of paper. Then the paper tore and the pencil point broke.

I howled and wept. Tears, mucus, and spittle poured down my face. I held my breath and buried my face in my hands, balling my fists and knuckling them into my eyeballs. How could I try so hard and feel so miserable? I dug my fingernails into the palms of my hands and tore at my clothes. I willed myself to be quiet, but keening wails escaped my lips.

Father Abraham knocked on the door of my room, which we'd painted spring green to my specification. When he opened and closed the door, the white eyelet curtains sucked in and blew through the open window. Strange to remember those details now, especially since the demon robs me of color.

"What's wrong, Carole?" My father's voice was quiet, low, and gentle.

"I don't know, Daddy. I don't know, I don't know… I just. Don't. Know."

My father listened for a while, but there was nothing he could do. Since my mind had narrowed to a pencil-point, only senseless babble came out of my mouth. After Daddy left, I climbed under my bedcovers, pulled into a tight ball, and toughed out the blinding headache.

The next day, I donned a mask of merriment, what I called "my happy face." The show must go on. Until the next all-consuming, colorless crash.

I sat in the den, staring at Gretchen's psychologist's report. *What does this mean? Why am I thinking about this now?* I hadn't had a panic attack in years and certainly hadn't told anyone about them, not even Keith. *No secrets,* he'd said. Except. *It's okay to hide a poisonous demon to prevent its resurfacing, isn't it? To protect myself and Keith. But could I keep this from him and still consider myself honest? And there was more to tell. Much more. If I told him my secrets, would he still love me?*

My chest tightened. *What should I do? Do what you usually do,* I told myself. *Push it aside, change the subject, and forge ahead.* I tucked Gretchen's psychologist's report into the folder and returned the file to the cabinet upstairs. Out of sight, out of mind. Nothing to be done. A dodge, I knew. But when faced with literal housebuilding and the metaphor, I chose the former, because literal was something I could do.

Our builder had responded to my email about appliances with a request for paint colors for each room. When renovating the townhouse, I'd discovered Keith possessed an uncanny intuition about what shapes and colors worked well together. So, after he got home, changed clothes, and settled in his chair in the living room, I handed him the paint chart deck.

"Which color for our bedroom?"

He fanned the deck, stared intensely for a few seconds, and pointed. "That one." Unlike my shades-of-beige choices, his bold decisions—mint green, sky blue, rose-orange, and gold—worked perfectly. Even I could see that.

I gave him a thank-you hug and kiss, then said, "I suspect Gretchen got her art and architectural abilities from you." Keith had designed our mountain house on graph paper.

"Design was one of Gretchen's strengths as an artist," he said. "She also shared my curiosity. Wherever I went, she always wanted to go. Always." Another familiar story. I waited for nuance.

"She was my daughter." His voice softened. "My darling daughter."

I snuggled close to his memories and felt a sweet closeness to mine—wonderful times with my children and the good work I'd done as a teacher. But the sweetness shifted as the morning's troubling questions resurfaced. I chewed my bottom lip. It's okay not to burden people with the hard parts of life, isn't it? And I'd made it, hadn't I?

I know, I know, go into danger, I said to the Spirit within. The only dangerous thing I'd done in the past six months was to tell Keith about my attempted murder of a grasshopper, which felt small in comparison. Couldn't I go into safety to find safety?

If I'd been paying attention, I would have noticed. The Spirit remained silent.

Chapter 11

Flooring

I gazed out the den windows on the main floor of our Alexandria townhouse one early-spring morning and watched the neighbor kids, slouching under backpacks, trudging to the bus stop in the sleepy, rose pink dawn. Puppies, I sighed, as I'd been at their age, and it's someone else's turn to teach them. Though I'd applied for jobs and was getting some nibbles, I suspected my thirty-four-year career was over. Part of me didn't feel right about leaving my profession and neglecting my gifts. Another part of me knew I was holding on because I feared both the uncertainty of "what's next" and confrontation with "what was."

Why couldn't I move forward, as I always had? I rubbed the back of my neck. Keith and I had selected floorings, hickory and tiles, and there wasn't much more to do. Even though other things on my list—Gretchen, myself, Heathcliff—were taking longer than planned, that didn't seem enough. How to find my next mission? I decided to go into the safety of my first reinvention to find guidance.

A few days before, I'd searched my second-floor closet and found the journal I'd kept while student teaching. The journal was course-required, not personal like Gretchen's. In mine, I chronicled the students' challenges and my successes and failures with as much honesty as I could, knowing the supervising professor would be my witness. Skimming the entries, I marveled at how a green, twenty-one-year-old college student had transformed into a teacher. Given the state I was in six months prior, I thank God for that transformation.

The night before faculty orientation, I had not been able to sleep. Early the next morning, I donned a skirt, blouse, pantyhose, and low heels—

my attempt to look like a schoolteacher. I drove in my parents' '63 Ford Falcon station wagon to the nearby high school where I'd been assigned. Nine student teachers met in the Main Office before 8:00 a.m. We signed in and waited with our supervising professor in the Women's Faculty Room while teachers and staff voted on contracts. I noted the faculty rooms segregated by gender in the old, two-story brick-and-glass building but didn't say anything.

When summoned after 9:00 a.m., we trooped down the main floor hallway, which smelled of plastic paint and disinfectant, just like every school building I'd ever been in, including my college dorm. We joined the teachers for breakfast in the cafeteria. My stomach growled and roiled at the new set of smells—cooking grease, tater tots, and overcooked vegetables. I waved no thank you when offered a cinnamon bun.

The general faculty meeting started after 10:00 a.m. with routine agenda items, including introductions of new teachers, interns, and student teachers. We stood when our names were called. Everyone looked us over, summing us up with audible "oohs and aahs." I managed not to shake out of my shoes when introduced. After sitting, I folded my hands in different positions, trying to find a confident pose. Can I do this? What if I fail?

The superintendent stepped to the podium and spoke about summer programs, giving special attention to remedial reading. A quiet hum relaxed my body. There were real problems in this school and students who needed assistance.

At that moment, I found my mission. I vowed to help my students learn, to give them a chance in a world that could be cruel and hard for the poorly educated and those without study skills. Though I experienced a few nervous moments during my career, I never again felt anxious as a teacher. And I never gave up on my students. Ever. I focused on what they needed and designed lesson plans accordingly.

The first week, I observed my supervising teacher's classes and checked guidance records. My students ranged from gifted to remedial to troubled, with home problems, police records or on probation. The greater high school community's issues were all too real: rural poverty, child and substance abuse, juvenile delinquency, teen pregnancy. One of my students had had a baby the year before. I could close my eyes and see her, a seventeen-year-old silent slip of a girl with straight blonde hair and China doll eyes.

FLOORING

After a week of classroom observation, I stood in front of two classes of those students: a small catchall elective called Area Studies and a raucous group of twenty-seven juniors in U.S. History-Government. Student confidence was low and attendance poor. I armed myself with learning goals, behavioral objectives, instructional strategies, materials, assessments—and was totally unprepared. Yet, amid mishaps, missteps, and mistakes, I heard the quiet hum a few times, what I'd later recognize as grace.

Friday, November 17, 1972. The last day of student teaching. At the end of both classes, I gave a prepared speech. "I enjoyed teaching you and getting to know you as students, and I hope you learned at least a fraction of what you taught me." Then I walked down the main hall and out the front door. Returning to the college campus that day, I felt totally bereft. My final journal entry read: "I'm really going to miss teaching and really miss the students!!"

I looked out the den window into the mid-afternoon sun. Middle school kids bounced off the school bus and jostled one another along the sidewalk. Boys smacked sticks against our split-rail fence while girls linked arms with one another, giggling and pointing. I chuckled at their antics. Boys and Girls. God's plan for me? After one year in a co-ed public junior high school, I spent thirty-three years teaching adolescent girls in Catholic independent schools. Girls with China doll eyes like Jessica, Gretchen, and the adolescent mother from my student teaching. Searching, vulnerable, questioning, hopeful. For twenty-five years at Ursuline Academy of Dallas and eight years at Notre Dame Preparatory School in Maryland, I heard the quiet hum many, many times.

Heathcliff nudged my arm. 4:00 p.m. I picked up keys, leash, treat pouch, and poop bags.

We rounded the sidewalk, greeted José and Princess, romped in the dog run—no Buddy this time—and headed home. Heathcliff walked loose-leash and in step to my left. At the entrance to the playground, beside the bench, a group of six or seven middle school boys I'd never seen before hung around a bigger boy. He held a light-grey pit bull puppy against his chest. The blue-eyed pup, which couldn't have been more than two months old, snuggled his head under the boy's chin.

I saw the boy smirk as he held the puppy away from him. Then he slapped its face. The pup yipped and cried. Heathcliff whimpered and shied. His big body pressed against my leg while his head wobbled back and forth between me and the pup. The other boys looked down, scuffed the dirt with their sneakers, and laughed nervously.

The boy grinned and slapped the puppy's face again. My gut roiled. The beast.

Heathcliff looked at me and cried, and my heart rose in my chest. I stroked Heathcliff's ear and cooed. "It's okay, Boy, it's okay, nobody's going to hurt you."

Even though the boys outweighed and outnumbered me, there was no question about what I had to do. A force greater than myself precluded my beastly fear. I'd experienced this feeling many times in my career, placing myself in harm's way to protect students from themselves. But now, in addition to the boys and the puppy, I had Heathcliff's unpredictable behavior to consider. With both hands, I cinched his leash close, hoping the two of us would stay calm. I approached the big boy, planted my feet, and made eye contact.

"Don't hurt your puppy." I projected my teacher voice to the group.

Nervous laughter ceased. The big boy's eyes dropped to his feet, and he shuffled. I noted his baby fat. A big puppy. Probably doing to his little pup what had been done to him. Equating meanness with strength.

"I am a teacher," I said, regaining his eyes.

Tightening my grip on Heathcliff's leash, I took a deep breath, and delivered the lesson. "If you want your puppy to become a good dog, teach him to watch and walk beside you. Teach him to sit, lie down, stay, wait, and come." I softened my voice. "Take care of your dog, and he will love and guard you." I waited a few beats then turned with Heathcliff by my side.

On the way home, I prayed the boys had sensed God's grace rather than my anger and fear. Then I remembered what Keith had said about Gretchen and small creatures. Like scattering seeds, we never know how well a lesson might take. Would the God-given seeds I'd scattered bounce off the dusty pavement or take root in the boys' hearts and minds? I hoped for the latter.

While cooking dinner, I conversed with the Spirit. It's not lost on me what happened today. When I chose the safety of my successful past, you led me into a dangerous confrontation. From now on, I'll go where you guide me. Into the heart of danger to confront my fearful past.

Chapter 12

Accessories

Heathcliff and I visited Mother again later that spring. Same routine: let ourselves in, kiss hello, make tea and decaf, catch up on the news, lapse into the comfort of silence. As an elementary school teacher, Mother had scattered many seeds among her students. Now she picked up a seed from the past and shared it with me.

"You know the other day, I was waiting to pick up a prescription at the pharmacy. This old man with a cane approached me. 'You're Joyce Duff, aren't you,' he said, and I nodded. 'I was one of the doctors who did your surgery. It was our first limb reattachment.' Can you imagine, running into him after all these years?" Mother's voice rose to a dangerous pitch.

I uncurled my legs, placed my feet on the floor next to Heathcliff, and leaned forward. A detail about the unspeakable "accident." I leaped at the opening.

"That's amazing, Mother. Did you know yours was their first limb reattachment?" She shook her head. "I guess God was really watching out for you." My mother lived, I'm so lucky to have her. Then I thought about what the two of us had been spared but had never acknowledged: I did not see her dying in her own blood.

"God was watching out for all of us," I said.

I saw Mother's lips thin. She looked away. "Maybe."

In her "maybe" I heard Mother's answer to my childhood question about the existence of God. "Maybe there is and maybe there isn't," spoken in a singsong voice. God the accessory.

God was never an accessory or a maybe for my Father Abraham. He'd rejected the religious legalism of his youth and made no secret of it. I recalled the Sunday morning when I was probably seven, and it was my turn to accompany him to the hospital and wait while he saw his patients. Mother encouraged my father to find opportunities to spend time with each of us. After what seemed like a long time, Daddy burst through the hospital corridor door into the Doctors' Waiting Room with an abrupt, "Let's go." On the drive home, he didn't talk about what happened—he didn't say anything—and I didn't ask. He had explained to us during dinner conversations about how he took care of sick children; and when there was nothing he could do to help them, he felt sad. But this wasn't sadness.

Daddy fiddled with the AM radio tuner. Jerking the dial past radio stations playing Sunday church services, he gritted his teeth. "Ha! Ha! Ha! God is dead, there is no God."

Our black '49 Chevrolet sped along Whalley Avenue and up Amity Road, Daddy's foot heavy on the gas pedal. I looked sideways at my father. His hands gripped the steering wheel.

An explanation formed in my mind: God is Dead and Daddy's angry and I am on my own. I gritted my teeth and pretend-laughed, too. Like father, like daughter. Maybe.

The light in the living room faded as the sun fell below the horizon. I wasn't seven anymore, and God was not dead, nor a maybe, nor an accessory. God is love.

I leaned closer to Mother. "Think of all the people your operation helped, all the successful limb reattachments those doctors did after yours." I wanted her to experience the mysterious joy, too. Maybe I also wanted her approval of me and my faith.

"I guess," she said, still refusing to look at me.

I'd made my point three times—stated, restated, reworded— like a good teacher. No need to belabor the point. I pulled the window shades down and turned on the inside lights.

"What would you like for supper?" I asked.

"How 'bout going to Teddy's." Teddy's was a family restaurant in Bethany, about a five minutes' drive.

"Do you think Mrs. Taffel would like to go, too? We could swing by and pick her up." Unlike me, Mother's dear friend Helen Taffel had not been spared the sight of blood on the day of "the accident." Her family had lived on Sanford Road at Newton. In the 60s, they built a house

ACCESSORIES

across the valley from ours, off Seymour Road where Mrs. Taffel now lived alone and no longer drove due to her failing eyesight.

"Let's take Helen to lunch at *The Gathering* tomorrow." The Gathering was their favorite little lunch-cafe. "I'll call her when we get back and ask if she'd like to go."

As Mother collected her cane, Heathcliff jumped up, wagging his tail. "Wait," I said to him. "Stay and guard." Heathcliff slumped on the living room carpet and sighed.

"If we go now, we'll be home in time for *Wheel of Fortune* and *Jeopardy*," Mother said. "Then dessert in front of *Murder, She Wrote*. I do love Angela Lansbury. She's so clever."

On the drive home to Alexandria with Heathcliff, I asked myself why I kept changing the subject. Who was I protecting, Mother or myself? Probably both, Mother from her anxiety and me from another unspoken part of "the accident." I was an accessory, an accessory to the crime. My real secret. Best to keep that locked away because secrets hide both angels and beasts—both terrifying.

As we passed through the tollbooth at the end of the New Jersey Turnpike and drove the short distance to the Delaware Memorial Bridge, I remembered another passage from Gretchen's short story "Rain." The protagonist had lied to her lover, promising never to leave him. "Transparent, but it's always been like that, hasn't it?" she wrote. "If you tell the truth, you're dead. They'll kill you. Saint John, Jesus Christ himself..."

The rhythmic *thunk-thunk* of tires hitting the bridge's expansion joints created an ominous beat as Gretchen's words looped in my head. *If you tell the truth, you're dead. If you tell the truth, you're dead. If you tell the truth, you're dead.* I imagined expansion joints opening and cars plunging into the Delaware River visible below. Though fearful, I felt no ambivalence. Unlike the Wilson Bridge crossing ten months before, I wanted to see the danger.

We sailed through the E-ZPass and were on solid ground again. Perhaps I was made of sterner stuff than I thought. I'd faced disapproval three times. Keith didn't hate me when I told him about the grasshopper; no one got hurt when I confronted the puppy-slapping boy; and I hadn't died when I told Mother the truth about my faith. Through the heart of danger into safety.

For the remainder of the trip, I pondered the future. The mountain house was nearing completion with installation of the accessories we'd selected. Thus, ended my part-time job. With no teaching offers in sight, I decided to extend my "sabbatical" for another year. I rather enjoyed the freedom to choose what I wanted to do, and there was plenty: two houses, one dog, two parents—Mother in Connecticut and Keith's dad in southern Virginia—plus more to learn about Gretchen as a young adult. Her journal and the nagging "maybe" about trust. I decided on a new focus for my reading—faith. And if plenty wasn't enough, I'd make it enough.

I'd earmarked Richard Rohr's *Falling Upward: A Spirituality for the Two Halves of Life* for summer reading. No matter how much I clung to it, the first half of my life was ending. So, I decided to find out what I needed to do to rebuild myself for the second half.

Looking back, I see the choice to explore the next stage of life marked a shift in my quest. An exciting opportunity to try new things. And dangerous for someone who's waiting at the threshold because she doesn't know who she really is.

Part II: Moving to Vanaprastha

To come to be what you are not, you must go by a way in which you are not.
-John of the Cross, The Ascent of Mount Carmel

Chapter 13

Re-missioning

Vanaprastha means forest dwelling, the third of four stages in Hindu life. It's a transition between Grihastha, work-family household living, and Sanyasa, detachment at the end of life. Vanaprastha is the name that Keith and I gave to our mountain home, a place for retreat then retirement, or as we called it, "re-missioning." What new mission was I supposed to be doing?

From the beginning of my sabbatical, while reading Gretchen's journals and listening to Keith's stories, I had also written about her. With Keith's encouragement, I added a book project to my "plenty-to-do" list. In retrospect, writing about Gretchen was safer, one step removed, less honest compared to writing about myself. But at the time, her story felt dangerous because of our strange connection points, which leaked through the pages. Two little girls' encounters with insects, mental health episodes in adolescence, Gretchen as my student, my daughter, me. Despite these mysterious parallels, I forged ahead and signed up for a marketing class titled "Social Networking for Writers" held at The Writer's Center in Bethesda, Maryland.

On Saturday morning, about a dozen people gathered in the Center's experimental theater, aptly named since most of us were experimenting and trying to act like writers. I mounted the tiered steps and took a seat in the second row, off to the side. My choice of location betrayed how I felt: no longer worthy to be front and center.

The young instructor, seated below us on stage, glanced up from her cell phone and explained she was checking her Twitter feed. She could have been one of my students—one of my recent students. The instructor told us her name, professional background, and class goals.

"Now introduce yourselves, and in one word or phrase or sentence tell us what you're writing."

I chewed my lip.

"Who would like to go first?" the instructor asked. "Give us your elevator speech." Elevator Speech? She must have noticed the puzzled looks on our faces because she added, "You know, three minutes about who you are, what you're writing, and why people want to read it—like pitching to an agent or speaking to your target audience."

Target Audience? I slunk down in my seat hoping the instructor wouldn't call on me. That behavior had never worked for my students when I was the teacher, but I slouched anyway. Thank goodness, someone volunteered and pitched a nonfiction project in her area of professional expertise.

"Excellent." Our instructor looked around the room. "How about the rest of you?"

Silence again until another member of the class spoke up. "I'll go next, but I don't have a pitch."

"That's okay, just tell us who you are."

When it was my turn, I said, "Carole Duff, former teacher, writing a memoir, I think..." I took copious notes during the class without absorbing much. Still, I learned something valuable: I didn't know who I was or what I was writing about or why anyone would want to read it.

The following month, I enrolled in an eight-week course for writers of literary nonfiction, taught in the evening by an instructor about my age. As a veteran history and social studies teacher, I'd taught my students the five-paragraph essay and other academic writing—deductive, expository, and researched-based. Since I was also a published technical writer in education, I felt confident literary nonfiction would be a natural step toward reinvention. Writing is writing. Right?

Early one hot, sticky night in June, we sat around the table and read through an excerpt I thought represented my best work. My first submission. The story of five-year-old Gretchen, whose perfect world ended when her parents divorced, and hints about my same-age loss.

"Who is the protagonist?" a classmate asked after we all finished reading. I'd never written much about myself and didn't know in memoir the protagonist is always the narrator, the author, me.

So, I said, "All will become clear later in the book," thinking I was supposed to answer questions. I didn't know the "cone of silence" rule of workshopping yet.

"What is the plot, the conflict, the story arc?" Questioning persisted, as did my parrying.

"Carole, be quiet and listen," our teacher said. I wanted to clutch the printed pages to my chest and weep. Thank goodness my desperate need to save face held back the tears.

"Why did you write this? What is the story really about?" Everyone seemed to know how to play this game except me. I felt like a kid who'd been chosen last for a sports team, limping to the end of the line.

"I guess I still don't know," I murmured. Yet another unknown, including the fact that not knowing is typical for memoir writing, particularly in the early stages.

To conclude the workshop, the instructor asked if I had any questions. "No," I said then added, "thank you for your feedback," hoping to rescue myself from complete humiliation. In truth, I was far from grateful. I had hoped for and expected accolades, like I'd received as a veteran teacher, but now feared I would not succeed as a writer.

On my drive home to Alexandria, cloud-to-cloud lightning from an approaching storm streaked across the night sky. I gripped the steering wheel and attended to the road while self-pity and failure rained down on me: you're not good at this kind of writing. Inductive. Personal. Beyond the realm of rational control. For over three decades, I'd been a front-and-center sage on the stage and guide on the side. Now I was nothing.

Why does it have to be this way? I asked God. *What do you want from me?*

I parked in our numbered space, grabbed my belongings, and ran through pouring rain toward our townhouse. Heathcliff greeted me at the door with his hopping dance. He followed me upstairs and, fearing the thunder, curled in his nest bed on the carpeted floor of our bedroom. With storms rattling outside our house and inside my head, sleep was a long time coming.

The next morning, Keith poured me a cup of coffee while I made his lunch. "How'd it go last night?" he asked.

"I thought I knew how to write," I whined. "But I don't have a clue what I'm doing..."

"That's what creativity feels like, Sweetheart. You're a novice again. Have fun with it."

I heard Keith's coaching words from our weight workouts together: Grunt it up.

"Yes, yes, I know, just like student teaching." I sighed and handed him his lunch.

Both of us had chosen intellectually demanding careers. We'd decided to build our house on the side of a mountain because the forest was a challenging place to live. Though physically declining—we weren't young adults anymore—growth in all aspects of life was our focus. That meant showing up prepared, learning as much as possible, being good citizens by supporting others' work, and contributing to the community.

I attended every class. If nothing else, I would get my money's worth, an easier goal to target than figuring out what my story was really about. I didn't know I was living the story or that Gretchen was my guide. But I did know I wasn't ready to reveal my secrets.

Not yet.

In addition to the weekly writing classes, I signed up for another Saturday marketing class titled Writers' Platforms taught by the same young instructor. Though I didn't have a pitch yet, I prepared an introduction. "I'm a former teacher, transitioning to literary nonfiction writing—personal essays and memoir," I said. "I'm interested in writing about life cycles, nature, and their seasons."

After preliminaries, our instructor said, "Social networking is marketing, and it begins and ends with a blog." So, we were back to social networking again, I thought, and blogging. That I thought I could do. When she asked us to make a list of possible topics, I wrote: dogs, death, divorce, adolescence, bipolar and other mental disorders, Al-Anon, single parenting, partnership, mission, the geography of childhood, aging, complaining—that I knew I could do.

The class was jam-packed with new information. I scribbled notes as fast I as could. Blog sites. Websites. Business cards. Fan pages on Facebook. YouTube. Twitter. Newsletters. Email lists. Podcasts. Nonfiction book proposals. Promotions.

Lions and tigers and bears. I was Dorothy in the strange land of Oz.

"I also teach an advanced class in blogging," our instructor said at the end of class. "But I don't want to see any of you signed up until you've been blogging for a while."

Marching orders. The next day, I registered for a free WordPress site. I called my blog *Notes from Vanaprastha*, our forest retreat, the second half of life.

Click—Publish. In a fit of narcissism and nerves, I posted my first blog titled "Father's Day." What if the world doesn't like what I wrote? I worried. I needn't have. According to my site statistics, hardly anyone read that first post, except my mother and only because I emailed the text to her. She said she loved it.

Eventually, I established a once-a-week, Monday posting schedule. I wrote to think; I wrote to practice; I wrote to hold my feet to the fire and publish. My blog was a personal journal made public, a hugely courageous new thing for me to do. Because for the first time in my life I was writing about myself. Because I had promised to write whatever the Spirit told me to write. Because as soon as I clicked "Publish," the post was out there for anyone to see.

No more secrets. Could I trust myself to do that? Yes, on that mission, I could.

Chapter 14

Anniversaries

On the Summer Solstice, Keith and I wished Alex a happy birthday, and I marked the fifteenth anniversary of Daddy's death. In truth, Father Abraham had died ten years earlier, felled by a right-brain stroke. June 22nd was the tenth anniversary of Gretchen's death, and three days later, our fifth wedding anniversary. A birthday, two deaths, and a wedding, four life-stage events within five days. We planned to celebrate our anniversary at Vanaprastha over the Fourth of July—two years after vacationing at Blackwater Falls where I had first tried to read Gretchen's journals.

We visited the mountain house twice in May, first to check plumbing, electric, heating, cooling, and paint. Then in late May for bathroom and kitchen fixtures, countertops and cabinets, tile flooring and wood stoves. Instead of ladders, stairs connected the main floor with the basement and loft. Heathcliff security-checked every room then lay down in the dusty loft within view of the French doors at the front of the house.

In Alexandria, Heathcliff and I observed the little blue-eyed pit bull, romping around the playground. Though I witnessed no more slaps, the incident caused a Heathcliff-like vigilance in me. While awaiting the certificate of occupancy for our mountain house, I transcribed passages of Gretchen's first three journaling books in order to chronicle her story and make sense of duplicate entries, overlapping dates, and poetry—both original and copied—scattered among and within the entries. In the process, I discovered an entry I hadn't read before.

I do not believe in coincidences.

* * *

August 8, 1998: "Last night he visited, and we went for a walk. It was electric between us, as I have not grown accustomed to. Really electric—I touched his arm and a spark leaped between our two separate limbs, and so we laughed. I was thinking of circuits, and how many things can be described as 'flowing'. We 'flowed' back to my place, where we sat around. He began to poke at me with his index finger, and we roughhoused a bit, all limbs and rolling around. He stopped and looked at me. He hit my face. I thought, "an accident." He did this twice more. Smiling. A rictus smile. He was still looking into my eyes. I wanted to cry, frantically, and laugh, hectically. I think I went a little crazy inside. I said, "You can leave anytime you feel ready," in a very friendly tone. I smiled calmly and brightly.

"And he left. I paced around my apartment in a tight little circle and did not do those things I was doing inside. My fierce agitation has not yet quit, not really. And I haven't heard from him. No man has ever before struck me for any reason. I thought precariously that this sort of thing took place in a rampage of chaotic action, sort of like scrambled eggs hurled through the air, running down the wall. I'd thought this sort of thing left more evidence, a stain, at least. But it was not like this at all. It was very brief and ordered. I could easily pretend it never happened at all...

"Some people like to tie up heads and hearts as well as bodies. I think of this in a distant way, thinking of it like I'd toy with a sausage link I don't intend to eat. Meanwhile, the eggs are on the wall; and if I get too close to thinking of it, in a personal way, my breath becomes like sort of a wail, and I close my eyes, hang my head. I never saw this, never could have predicted it. He hit me, he hit me and he was smiling! I wonder if he does secretly enjoy it. I wonder if he doesn't have a better use for me than this."

* * *

I recoiled as if I was the one who'd been slapped. How could he do that to her? Why did she let him get away with it? Better use? How could she think she should hide what happened? Where was the fearless girl Keith had told me about, the six-year-old who jumped off the high-dive at the community pool? The ten-year-old and only girl in her Tae Kwon Do class, the only student to kick through the board? A girl after my own heart, I the resident daredevil and neighborhood tree-climbing champ, the only person to summit The Big Maple. Where was the courageous girl I wanted her to be, the girl who knew the slap wasn't "an accident?"

Accident. I closed my eyes. An accident. That's what I called the attack on my mother, which was a big pretend because the attack was not an accident—maybe the first time I'd admitted this. Why had I denied the truth, like Gretchen had? So, I wouldn't have to admit there are people who do those terrible things. So, I wouldn't get too close and go crazy. So, I wouldn't wail then close my eyes and hang my head. So, I wouldn't die of shame.

If you tell the truth, you're dead—Gretchen's warning echoed, and I replied, oh, but I would never let someone treat me like that. Then I remembered what my mother's friends said about what had happened to her. Sometimes the stories we tell to comfort ourselves also make us more vulnerable. Did I know how I'd react if someone I loved didn't have better use for me? Yes, I did, on the morning my first husband left. This time I remembered the scene not in anger but in truth, because my response to his leaving was the same as Gretchen's. We both pretended everything was okay and did not say what we were thinking.

My first husband sat at the foot of our bed, dressed for work but in no hurry. Outside, the Texas summer shimmered with jalapeño heat and cicadas, rattling in the backyard. I'd lined up chores for the day—cleaning up from the previous night's dinner party, driving our children to dance workshops and community day camps, preparing for my graduate class in educational administration—but put my checklist on hold when I breezed into our bedroom and noticed his slump. He usually managed even heavier-than-usual drinking, so this was likely something else.

"What." I stopped in front of him.

He lifted his head. "I want my own apartment. I want my own credit card. I want to find true love before it's too late."

True love? What am I, chopped liver? I asked myself. What does he think I've been doing all these years? Nothing?

I broke out in a cold sweat and shivered. This can't be happening. Divorce is something that happens to other people, not to me. And yet, I understood his desire. Both of us spent a great deal of time away from home, working days, nights, and weekends, and I'd filled the family calendar with our children's activities and social events. Without time alone together, our partnership and intimacy had dwindled to almost nothing. In truth, my kids-come-first busyness helped me ignore the fact that we hadn't been rowing our marital boat in the same direction for a long time. Now we weren't even in the same boat. After sixteen years of marriage, we needed to decide between a bad choice, splitting up, and a worse one: staying together.

He leaned forward. "I'll come for Sunday dinner, you cook, and we'll be a family."

I lowered my voice almost to a whisper. "If you leave, we won't be a family."

Apparently, my words were not what he wanted to hear because he jerked to his feet and strode into the living room toward the front door.

"What did I do wrong?" I trailed him with pleading hands. What more could I have done to earn his love without losing my soul?

"You're too controlling. You work too hard which makes people nervous. You're not a good hostess." Even though my gut vehemently denied everything he said, my heart knew he was right on the last point. When entertaining, I was more comfortable hiding in the kitchen like Lazarus' sister Martha rather than engaging my guests in the living room like their kind-hearted sister Mary. Someone had to do the work. Right?

I clenched my teeth. "Go."

"Our marriage takes more than your commitment," he said, as if I needed reminding.

I wanted to say, "What about you, Buddy?" but he'd closed the front door behind him.

Pacing the living room floor in endless circles, I wondered how we could have come to this. People fought and threw things and went on rampages. But our split was very brief and ordered. And not something I could pretend never happened.

We agreed to separate, and he moved out in mid-August. The day before our sixteenth wedding anniversary, two days before David's eighth birthday, two weeks before my fortieth birthday and his forty-third. We divorced the following year, a week after Jessica's twelfth birthday. Four birthdays, the death of a marriage, and years of would-have-been wedding anniversaries.

I sat in the den and puzzled. Why hadn't I said what I was thinking until it was too late? Why didn't Gretchen? She and her boyfriend had been roughhousing. Did he think she wanted to be slapped or he could get away with mistreating her? She didn't do anything except smile and say, "You can leave anytime you feel ready." And then he left. Did my ex-husband think I would be fine with what he was saying to me? If I'd said what I was thinking during our years together, our marriage might have been better—or ended a lot sooner.

Maybe that's why I hid in the kitchen. If I said what I was thinking, people might not like me for who I am. And loved ones, who didn't have better use for me, might leave.

Chapter 15

Two Professions

Keith and I packed the Subaru with supplies to camp out over the Fourth of July weekend in the house we'd built together. We'd received our certificate of occupancy for Vanaprastha. As I had on our Blackwater Falls vacation two years prior, I took along Gretchen's journals. I've heard engineers only learn from failure because anything better means doing the same thing with maybe a little tweaking. In life, I'm an engineer. Or maybe I needed to step back and ponder what "better use" meant before embracing my new profession, my new occupation. In any case, we arrived before sunset, unpacked, ate the turkey cobb salad I'd prepared, made up our bed, laid out Heathcliff's in the great room, and retired for the night.

The next morning, we woke like starry-eyed newlyweds in our forest love nest. New hickory floors gleamed in the unobstructed sunlight shining through our windows—no drapes, curtains, or shades, only mountains, trees, and sky. Heathcliff frolicked outside then sprawled on the cool floor in the great room. The house placed us in the natural world while protecting us from its dangers.

Our furniture consisted of two metal folding chairs, a Coleman ice chest, which doubled as a bench, a rack of four wooden TV tables, a full-sized aerobed, two beanbag chairs, and my maternal Grammy's rocking chair. This is home, I thought as I sat in one of the folding chairs on the deck next to Keith. This is home.

I remembered the first time I'd heard those three words. Fifteen years ago. While on vacation. In Virginia.

July 1996, six months after our baptism and one month after my father died, my children and I drove down 95 South from Dulles Airport toward Richmond, heading for Williamsburg and Busch Gardens. Jessica was sixteen and David twelve. Virginia's lush greenery, so different from Texas, lined the highway, and traffic swirled around us.

Then something wondrous happened. All sound and images faded except for the trees and sky. I smelled and heard their colors, hues of green and blue. Time and space seemed suspended. A gentle breeze from an unknown source caressed my face and raised the hair on my arms. I relaxed my hands on the steering wheel. An inaudible, deep voice boomed inside my head. *This is home. This is home.*

Hearing that voice—the loudest I'd ever heard—I woke as if from a reverie.

Who? What? How? I asked. The reality of 95 South returned. I told Jessica and David about the voice, what it said, and my astonishment. This is home? We live in Texas; we're on vacation. I don't remember my children having any reaction, except maybe, "Oh, Mom..." Compared to Busch Garden's Loch Ness Monster and Big Bad Wolf roller coasters, the voice I heard and the time lapse I'd experienced probably didn't seem like a big deal.

A few years later, I heard that voice again. I had invited a dear friend, a teaching colleague, to my house for a mini-Thanksgiving dinner of roast chicken with all the trimmings. At the end of the evening, we walked to her car parked along the curb.

I looked back at my Texas house. Again, all sound and imagery faded, except the front door of the house. I smelled the twilight and felt the gentle breeze. My body calmed, and time suspended. Then I heard the deep, booming voice in my head. *You will not be staying here.* The voice startled me, again. I told my friend, a believer. We both knew who it was, no question.

And so, I applied for jobs on the east coast, closer to Mother, while renovating and cleaning out my house. Keep. Pitch. Give away. When offered the position of Academic Dean at Ursuline Academy of Dallas, the job I'd wanted for years, I turned down the offer. Saying no thank you was surprisingly easy because I knew I was supposed to be somewhere else, though I had no idea where. In due time, I would know.

"This is home," I said to myself as I gazed across the Rockfish Valley to the Blue Ridge Mountains and Three Ridges Wilderness Area. A cool mountain breeze caressed my face and arms. Birds flitted among the tulip poplars; hawks and eagles circled above. "This is home."

Keith had set up his portable chess set on a TV table and was immersed in his game. I smiled at his contentment and mine. My mind settled into quiet reflection, recalling the circuitous route that had brought us together.

No coincidence.

After leaving Texas and moving to Baltimore with just our family's deaf old cat, I'd kept in touch with Jessica, working at a law office in Dallas, and David at college in New York City. The position at Notre Dame Preparatory School was everything I wanted: challenging work with dedicated colleagues and constant learning. After a few months, I applied for a scholarship to take graduate classes at Goucher College near NDP to learn new skills. I promised myself I would not fill my time with work alone but gave little thought to a social life or finding a church.

One morning at breakfast, following my God time walk, for some reason I turned to the obituary section of *The Baltimore Sun*—not my usual routine. There was a long write-up about a professor at Goucher. She had lost her fiancé in World War II and stayed home after the war to care for her aging parents. After they died, she enjoyed a successful career as a college professor. Never married, she was known for traveling with her two cats.

A cat lady? I wondered. Is that what I'm supposed to be?

Days later, a snowstorm hit the area, and my Saturday morning graduate class was cancelled. It kept snowing. I read books and shoveled a path to my neighbor's house to feed her cats while she and her family were away for the Presidents' Day weekend. It kept snowing. Schools closed and almost everything shut down, including local, state, and federal governments. And still it snowed. Somehow *The Baltimore Sun* arrived every morning. I read the newspaper cover-to-cover including the personal ads—also not my usual routine.

Maybe I'm not supposed to be a cat lady.

I signed up for the free trial period for an online dating site advertised in the newspaper and submitted my profile then poked around the site. Only one profile caught my attention: "…attending Shakespeare Theater…writing Dad's World War II stories… planning a mountain house…" I sent him an email.

A few dates into our courtship, Keith told me his side of our story. He'd cancelled his subscription and retracted the letter he'd posted to a different site, but not the one where I found him. Still without a partner, he prayed: "Lord, I'm not doing very well. I'm not making good choices. If you send me someone, I promise I'll follow-up on the next lead you send me."

When my email arrived that afternoon, his finger hovered over the delete key, because his online dating experience had been a disappointment. Then he laughed and remembered his promise. He opened the email and responded.

The following day, my heart ticked with curiosity as I opened his message and read: "You will find me very honest and reliable and direct." Honest, reliable, direct. Good. "I'm provocative in conversation, inquisitive, a good listener, and I do my homework. I don't respect anyone with a strong opinion on issues they know nothing about. If I feel an emotional reaction, but haven't done the research, I'll say that. Some of that is just me, an ENTJ, and some comes from being an intelligence analyst."

On the Myers-Briggs' personality inventory, I am more introverted (I) than extroverted (E), more sensing (S) than intuitive (N), more feeling (F) than thinking (T). And, like most teachers, a strong J for judgment. We had one trait in common, for better or worse.

Keith wrote, "I think I am a tough match for any woman, not what every woman wants. Probably too intense and not at all laid back, but several women have told me I was the most interesting man they knew. I'm sure I would not bore you; maybe exasperate you."

Ah, a challenge, I thought, how delicious! If I step up to this, I'll learn new things and grow, just as I was growing in the job at NDP.

We communicated by email through the storm—the Blizzard of 2003—both of us wondering if that had been planned, too. When Keith told me about Gretchen's death and Alex's struggles to recover from the loss, I offered to help. "Thank you," Keith wrote. "Women usually ask about my children then tell me good luck with that." We agreed on a date in early March to meet for dinner at the Rusty Scupper overlooking the Inner Harbor in Baltimore.

Before our first date, I tried on at least eight outfits. I hadn't dated in years and had never been good at it. Am I still attractive? I wondered. Are my teeth white enough? Ugh, adolescence revisited. Crossing the restaurant parking lot that Sunday evening, I scolded myself so I wouldn't cut and run. You. Will. Not. Stand up this man. My heart pounded as the hostess showed me to Keith's table. He stood and took my nervous hand in his. Such beautiful hands, I noticed, strong yet beautifully shaped. Later, I would wonder if Gretchen had her father's hands.

Over a sumptuous meal of oysters, salad, and grilled salmon, we talked about our families, missions and values, finances, and health—spiritual, intellectual, physical. We discovered a common resilience. At the age of two, Keith had contracted polio, which compromised his right leg as opposed to my clubfooted left. He was left-handed to my right. Walking side-by-side with our strong legs and dominant hands to the outside, we would bookend one another.

We also spoke of our successes, and otherwise. Honest and direct. No party-faces. "I'm not proud of my failures," Keith said, "and I've had many—and learned a lot from them." I sat still and listened carefully to this unusual man. "I've been married three times." A second marriage during his children's grade school years hadn't survived either. "It would be easy to blame my kids, but I couldn't leave them. I hold myself responsible for my children not doing well. My second and third wives were good women. They had no children of their own and wore themselves out trying to help me with Gretchen and Alex."

"I can understand that," I said, remembering my own struggles.

"Also, it's not easy being married to an intelligence analyst. I want to understand things. I was given the gift of discernment, and I'm confrontational." And I was not. This was, indeed, going to be a challenge.

Then he told me something I'd never heard from anyone before. "After my third divorce, I looked in the mirror and had one of those serious talks. I had to raise the bar for myself in order to be worthy of a worthy partner."

I'm worthy, I thought, and the staying type. My skin tingled. Oh yeah, I was flipping out—and wondering why the ladies in the casserole brigade at church hadn't snapped him up. Later, he told me that he was similarly wondering why I was available.

"Dessert?" he asked. "We could share—you said you liked to do that."

As the waitress poured coffee, he reached across the table to hold my left hand. "I'd like to pick up the tab. Would you mind?"

I stirred real cream into my coffee and savored the rich flavor. After four years with Jessica in college and now David, money was tight. Paying for my meal would have meant further belt tightening. And after going it alone for twelve years, his offer felt like a change I could get used to.

"Thank you so much, Keith, that would be lovely."

After dinner, he walked me to my car and turned. "So, are we having a second date?"

I hesitated. "I know you're looking for a partner, but I just moved here and don't know what I'm looking for." As I scanned his face, my entire being said without speaking: *Kiss me. Kiss me so I know your scent. Kiss me so I know your taste. Kiss me so I know you're the one.*

He leaned into my unspoken invitation.

Oh. My. Goodness. I am in So. Much. Trouble.

Lips flirted, dancing, laughing, singing. Then our kiss deepened and lingered. Not at all the person I thought I was yet truer than ever before.

Our profession of love and engagement followed a month later.

The sun beat upon the deck at Vanaprastha, and the breeze no longer cooled. We moved inside to the great room. Keith settled into a beanbag chair with a book, while I set up a folding chair with two TV tables for my laptop and Gretchen's journals. Heathcliff curled up between us. As Keith read, I transcribed until dinner and sundown, the end of our day at Vanaprastha. We knew we would not be staying here forever. Decline would overtake us, and we would join Gretchen and our parents in death. But for now, this was home.

That night, Keith and I stargazed, then went to bed, facing the large window in our bedroom. I wrapped my arm around him, spooning, our legs and feet entwined. As I rubbed my hands down his shoulders and back, he leaned into my familiar touch—a known thing.

Eros. Agape. Love. With someone who has better use for me and wants me for who I am. In this moment of intimacy in our new home, the thought dawned on me that moving into the third stage of life involved change in two professions: occupational, from a teacher's outer work to a writer's inner work, and personal, changes in my relationships, and I had work to do.

Chapter 16

A Third Way

Early the next morning, I startled into partial consciousness. Someone other than Keith was in the room. Squinting, I imagined seeing a small figure tucked in Grammy's rocker at the foot of the aerobed.

"Gretchen." I whispered in my dream.

She lingered then slipped one bare foot off the rocking chair and leaned toward me. "Love isn't like a favor or a trinket you could ask for to pin to your dress." She studied my face as if waiting for a response.

I gaped and puzzled. "Love is not an accessory, is that what you mean?"

She rocked back. "I wanted a lover like a foil for my character."

"Why a foil?"

"To experience life in different ways. Otherwise, I was only myself."

"Am I using you as a foil?"

She laughed softly. "A person's influence is temporary. But it's familiar, a known thing" With that, her image faded.

My encounter with Gretchen in a waking dream haunted me while I made breakfast and Keith tended to Heathcliff. Previous-day events often debriefed in my nightly dreams, so I knew the words she had spoken were from her journals. Where? I turned the burner with bacon sizzling on the stove down to low, washed my hands, scurried to our bedroom, and picked up her first journal. October 10, 1996. There—I pointed to the dream's words in her entry.

By the time I returned to the kitchen, the bacon had shrunk to dark, crisp strips. I lifted them onto a paper towel-lined plate, poured off the grease, and cracked three eggs into the pan. While the eggs cooked, I popped two slices of bread into the toaster, cut a fresh peach from the local Farmers Market, and set the TV tables for breakfast. Over-easy eggs fried brown and crisp around the edges.

After we sat down to eat, Keith forked the rock-solid yolks. "You overcooked the eggs."

"I'm not used to this cooktop; it's faster than the one in Alexandria," I said. Then more honestly, "I was thinking about a strange dream I had."

"Time sharing again."

I straightened. "Some people call it multitasking."

Keith's eyes locked on mine. "It's the brain toggling from one thing to another, then food gets overcooked."

"I know, I know, you don't have to criticize." I gritted my teeth so the angry words in my head wouldn't fly out of my mouth.

"It's not criticism, it's feedback." Keith frowned.

I frowned back at him. "It sure feels like criticism, and I'm hard enough on myself without you telling me."

He rolled his eyes and sighed. "I guess I can't ever give you any feedback."

An audible silence sizzled between us. Every fiber of my body tensed, resisting the impulse to bolt from the table, pack my bags, and run. Though I didn't have a clue where I'd go, I wanted to fly from this man who had challenged me from the start.

Nine months into our relationship, Keith and I were a starry-eyed engaged couple, enjoying our courtship's honeymoon stage. We still wore party faces during family visits and with our children. Alex lived with Keith in Alexandria; David lived with me in Baltimore during college breaks; and Jessica visited from Dallas.

Before my dear, cat-owning neighbors left for Christmas, I invited them to join us for dinner. I prepared a special meal, imagining scenes from Norman Rockwell's paintings on a Hallmark card. After dinner, my guests adjourned to the living room while I carried the leftovers into the kitchen. Keith and David got involved in a lively debate. To my ears, their discussion sounded like an argument, a confrontation.

I stuck my head into the living room. "Please stop," I said to Keith.

"Why? We're having a good time."

"Please change the subject to something more pleasant."

Keith ignored me. His and David's voices escalated. Upset about how this scene appeared to my neighbors, I asked Keith and David to stop arguing and change the subject—again. They both ignored me. I paced between the kitchen and dining room, torn between my future husband and beloved son, as if I had to choose to love one over the other. When I heard them shouting—that's what their discussion sounded like to me—I lost control and ran out the front door.

"I need a break." I tossed the words over my shoulder and slammed the door.

My feet pounded the neighborhood sidewalks, and soon the night chill cooled my temper. When I got back maybe twenty minutes later, Keith had left. I apologized to my neighbors and thanked them for coming. After a couple of hours—the average drive time to Alexandria—I called Keith at home.

"Why did you leave? I came back, and you were gone."

"I didn't think I was welcome." In his voice, I heard the toll of other leavings—friends, wives, his daughter. By walking out, I'd hurt him in the worst possible way.

"Of course, you are welcome. I just needed to cool off." Fear claimed my throat. "We were meant to be together, but maybe you're thinking not." I choked, and my voice trailed off.

We talked it out, as couples do, reviewing what happened from each perspective.

"I felt I needed to throw my body in front of David to protect him."

"David can take care of himself. He needed to be taken down a peg."

"Yeah, he's a sophomore and knows everything. When I told Mother, she said, 'Well, isn't it nice he knows everything, because it's the only time in life that will happen.'" I laughed.

We chatted for a while longer, then Keith said, "Don't worry, Sweetheart, we just had our first spat. Confrontation is good; it's problem solving. I'll see you tomorrow."

Over the years, there were more spats between us, some involving Keith and my children, who were accustomed to my indulgence and sometimes took advantage of my inconsistency. But now at Vanaprastha, the confrontation involved just the two of us, eating a silent, cold-shouldered breakfast. I made a conscious effort to calm my frightened heart and think.

Why does it have to be this way? I asked myself, then answered, because you're choosing it. When his comments sound like criticism, you choose the angry beast of self-defense and self-righteousness then sulk in self-pity and silence. Fight then flight. You avoid confrontation because to your ears and eyes, criticism is disapproval of you as a person. At least

I'd learned that much about myself in the past twenty years, since my first marriage failed.

We'd built this house together, and now I wanted to tear our house down because of overcooked eggs? He didn't hurl them through the air. They're not running down the wall. I got distracted and made a mistake. Why are mistakes so hard for me to admit?

Another thing I'd learned, in the past eight years with Keith was that we had opposite defaults when dealing with confrontation—mine in line with my family's avoidance and his consistent with his prickly nature. Even though I wanted him to stop, his ability to confront problems was one of the reasons I'd married him. And, unlike me, he didn't hold a grudge. He met problems face-to-face then moved on. Even though letting go of grudges wasn't my strong suit, as his partner, I could mirror that behavior. Not fight, nor flight. A third way.

"Do you have plans for today?" I asked as he cleared the dishes and loaded the dishwasher. "Would you like to explore this afternoon, maybe stop at a winery or brewery?"

"Sounds like fun. Let's do it."

On the drive back to Alexandria, after our weekend get-away, I thought about the spat with Keith and returned to the question I'd asked Gretchen in my dream. Was I using her as a foil? Yes, I guessed I was, to experience life in different ways and explore connections with her. Otherwise, I was only myself.

Who did I want to be?

A third way person who acknowledged her mistakes then let them go.

I'd finally asked the "be" question, though in my mind the third way was about doing something other than getting angry and running away. I now knew Gretchen was indeed my foil—my guide for this journey, though I didn't know my quest was about faith yet. I thought I had that figured out: listen and the Spirit will tell you what to do.

And so, I kept on doing, and God kept on being.

Chapter 17

No Accident

In Alexandria, I prepared for Hurricane Irene. Cars fueled, bottled water, nonperishable foods, flashlights and batteries, extra cash, charged cell phone, toiletries, medications, Heathcliff's food. If the storm headed for us, I would run a tub of water for flushing the toilet and bathing, as my family in Connecticut had done when I was growing up. Check, check, check. Everything under control.

My part-time job had ended in late July when Keith and I signed the closing papers for the conventional loan on the mountain house, but now I had two houses to maintain. In spare moments, I searched for a third way by reading Richard Rohr's *Falling Upward* for the first time and Gretchen's journals. The irony of seeking ways to let go while tightening control was totally lost on me.

That Tuesday in August was a mostly sunny day with temperatures in the low 80s. After our morning walk, Heathcliff slept beside me in the den. I felt emotionally strong enough to tackle the journal section I'd abandoned two years ago at Blackwater Falls, the part where I'd become dreadfully afraid and stopped reading. I backed up a couple of weeks to establish context and discovered another entry I must have skipped previously.

Or maybe I was meant to read this passage now.

* * *

> December 29, 2000: "Rich [snarky high school friend] drove me to my father's house on Friday night, following a strangely unpleasant episode. We'd been talking. He was

laughing at me and concluded with: 'You know, all the potential I imagined you had when we were in school is totally gone. I used to be able to see you adored or famous or wealthy. Now I can't even see you moving away from your stagnant life.' He mocked me. He laughed. I extended the middle finger of one hand. 'Can you see <u>this</u>?' I said, smiling. With my other hand, quick as that, I decked him across his soft face. He was bleeding; some satisfied thing in me ground its teeth. 'I guess you didn't see <u>that</u>, though.' Should we ever see each other again, there will be no wistful smile for roads not taken."

* * *

Not an "accidental" slap but a deliberate punch. Gretchen struck her friend because, though unsolicited, unkind, and likely influenced by his own feelings, he had told her a truth she had often written about but did not want to hear from others. She was stuck, afraid of success, afraid of her future. Rich had also mocked her for loving Harry, her former boyfriend. Gretchen's response was fight then flight, the two sides of fear, which I knew well. Hitting a grasshopper or a person feels natural and right, maybe even satisfying for a moment. Then comes shame, denial, and flight, because you're afraid of love, afraid of being rejected, afraid of being unlovable.

Don't stop, the Spirit whispered. *Keep going.*

I went into her fearful danger, praying I'd stay calm through what happened next.

* * *

January 8, 2001: "Last Friday, I went to a movie with Harry, but mostly I wanted to spend some time with him before I died. I'd intended to do the right thing and die, finally. It didn't really matter so much what we did; I just wanted a reminder of another simple thing I couldn't get right. Ugh. Who in their right mind would let me out into the world to make decisions?

"We had some words, I forget what was said and why, but we got into the car silently. I drained a wine bottle when he handed it to me; I thought about the small amount of beer I had at home. I thought I'd just have to find a knife. When he pulled up in front of the door, I thought, 'Please reach out to me, please stop me,' but he did not, and I got out.

"I reached my apartment thinking about the love I'd tossed out yet again, about the sex I wouldn't have that night or ever, and I took off my shoes. I ran the hot water in the sink, pulled up a chair, drained a couple of beers and began to slice. I couldn't find a vein. I thought I felt a happy pop once, and there was a jet of rusty fluid in the sink already foaming with dirty water.

"I thought I'd better call his answering machine to do an intent thing and make sure he got his stuff back. I thought he'd recognize my number and not answer. But he did, and somehow, I found myself saying what I always say: 'Help me, because I can't help myself.'

"Except this was the first time I'd ever said it to a person. He kept me on the phone and must have driven over like mad. I didn't know he was coming over. But he was standing in the door of my bathroom like I'd been cutting into him rather than myself, and his eyes were huge and shiny, and his jaw dropped. I wanted very much to vanish in a puff of stupidity.

"He kept saying, 'What am I going to do?' and I kept apologizing, mostly for making him think he had to do anything. All I thought of was, 'Too bad, too bad, why do I have to live, why the hell did he pick up the phone?'"

* * *

I marked my place in Gretchen's journal and took a deep breath. This time I recognized the all-too-familiar self-loathing for not getting things "right," though I didn't know what to do with that information yet. Instead, I focused on remembering what happened at Blackwater Falls. I'd read, "Help me, because I can't help myself," and her journal slipped from my fingers. Then I heard the scream from a long-ago nightmare inside my head. *Help, please, please help.* My recurrent dream had started after "the accident" that wasn't an accident. Though it had been fifteen years since I'd had that dream, I now recalled the nightmare in technicolor detail.

The dream began with the drone of a low-flying airplane followed by a booming crash. A large commercial airliner lay in the field beside the stone wall in front of my family's house. The plane had slammed into our vegetable garden. Beanstalks lay broken, vines scattered, and tomatoes oozed and bled. Red and yellow flames licked the plane's gleaming silver fuselage. Standing outside the breezeway door, I saw passengers strapped in their seats, arms outstretched, their faces begging. *Help, please, please help.*

Intense heat held me back. I watched from a distance, frozen. Time and again, I tried to run to them, to reach out, to say something, do something. Then I rewound the dream tape and tried to prevent the crash or rewrite a different, happier ending. But each time I woke from this loop-and-repeat nightmare with a deep sigh of failure.

No matter what I did or how hard I tried or how many times the scene replayed, dream after dream, night after night, I never rescued anyone. Not one person. Ever. There was the Gretchen connection: shame for not getting that right and guilt for failing to act.

I opened her journal. "Help me," she'd said. Too late, I murmured. I so much wanted to rescue you, Gretchen. I arrived too late. Too late. Too bad, too bad. Why did you have to die?

I squared my shoulders and read the rest of her entry.

* * *

January 8, 2001: "It wasn't exciting. You may look at endless despair with dewy-eyed, breathless yearning and think, 'How romantic.' I know people who do this; I've seen it. If you do this, you fail to understand exactly as I fail to know what to do to live. If you think this, you and I do not understand one another. Do not think there is anything sweet and romantic about needing to die to prevent further shame at your own worthlessness. Being useless is sad enough. Knowing that there may actually be a purpose to living and knowing with equal certainty that one is unable to accomplish that purpose, is as sad and dirty and ugly as searching for a vein with an X-Acto knife in the bathroom sink. If you look at this and think anything other than 'what the fuck' then you're kidding yourself. The duty of life is to not comprehend an urge toward death. If you <u>did</u> understand it, you would be there slicing yourself up right next to me, you would be tying rocks to yourself on a bridge, you would be setting yourself on fire in your bathtub and you would be reaching for your firearms. The duty of life is to <u>not</u> understand, to be confused and offended by it and thereby continue to live. I still live now for the same reason that I want to, need to die—because I am a failure. Rich was utterly correct in his assessment of the pointlessness of my existence; the fact that I struck the hell out of him for being right doesn't make him any less right. If you can make anything pretty out of this, you're much more ill than I."

* * *

I stared down at the floor. "No, there's nothing romantic about wanting to die, Gretchen. Nothing sweet about feeling useless, nothing pretty about failing to do your duty. I'm witness to that. No need to slap me, no need for rebuke. I understand." I marked my place again and stopped for lunch, needing time to refuel.

At 1:50 p.m., I was at my laptop in the den, transcribing Gretchen's entry. A minute later, the house shook. I checked the clock, walked through the kitchen, and looked out the window into the backyard. Everything shook.

"Dear God, I don't like this." I paced the main floor of the house, thinking I could magically hold the world together by watching the clock and pacing between the front door and back window. Clock, door, window. Clock, door, window.

Glassware jangled and plates rattled. Then the earth stilled. A plate in the dining room hutch wobbled, toppled, and broke. I turned on the news and called Keith.

"We're fine, Sweetheart. Yeah, we felt it here, too. Any damage?"

"Just a dessert plate, as far as I can tell. Heathcliff slept through the whole thing." I told Keith I'd call our builder and ask him to check the mountain house. All was well, the builder said. Out there, most people didn't even notice the quake. News stations reported damage but no deaths or serious casualties. Thanks be to God.

But if I had needed a humbling reminder that I was not in control, I sure got one. And what had I learned from Gretchen? Neither fight nor flight will make that truth any less true.

Chapter 18

Star Trails

Summer's heat yielded to autumn's cool. Keith and I opened the windows at our forest retreat Vanaprastha—a retreat, not retirement, not yet. We came to the mountain on weekends to enjoy gentle breezes and rustling leaves far from the roar of traffic.

One Friday evening, after dark, we lay on the futon that we had moved from Alexandria to Vanaprastha to replace the aerobed in our bedroom.

Keith stared out our bedroom window. "Did you say you saw a shooting star?"

"Not tonight, other times." I lazed toward his side of the bed.

"I must have been dreaming."

Looking into the dark night and stars over his shoulder, I softly hummed, "Vincent (Starry, Starry Night)"—Don McLean's ballad about Vincent van Gogh, one of Keith's favorite songs. Perhaps he was thinking about Gretchen, his shooting star.

My thoughts wandered to my own shooting star. Father Abraham. For my sixth-grade science project, he and I explored the heavens. On five clear, moonless nights, we pointed his Brownie box camera toward the sky, away from the light of the house. Daddy rigged the shutter to stay open so light passing through the lens's aperture captured time-lapse motion. Curved star trails across the dark heavens etched onto the film, empirical evidence of the earth's rotation happening right under our feet.

I'd found those photographs in my closet, stored in the original Yale Co-op processing envelope. Five prints tucked in a Snapshot Memories folder and wrapped in a scrap of beige writing paper on which my science teacher had written, "This is an excellent project." Through the years, whenever my eyes followed the star trails on those prints, I touched my father's magic once again and tasted our success: A. Perfection.

To meet the project due date, Daddy took photographs to use up the roll of film. There were two pictures of my sister Leslie, carrying her schoolbooks and dressed in her winter coat, tights, and tasseled stocking hat. Leslie must have taken the picture of Daddy holding his leather briefcase and standing next to the old Chevrolet, the driver's door open. The Chevrolet was featured in other pictures, one of them with the front yard's three maple trees and Daddy's homemade picnic table, all covered in a haze of January snow. The last shot captured a winter scene of our small backyard pond and the tire swing Daddy hung from the old hickory tree.

I stared into the starry-starry night at Vanaprastha. Only Leslie, the Connecticut house, one maple tree, and the pond remained. My father was gone.

The next morning after a successful eggs-over-easy breakfast, Keith set up his portable chess board and pieces on a TV table on the deck, as was his habit. Heathcliff ran the mountain behind the house, chasing squirrels, deer, and other critters and sniffing everything. He soon returned, panting and snorting his pleasure, with slobber strung across his muzzle. The drumming sound of a pileated woodpecker, foraging for insects in dead tree trunks, echoed across the valley, and goldfinches called *perchik-o-ree*.

"More coffee?" I held the carafe over Keith's cup.

"Yes, thank you, Sweetheart."

We sat side-by-side on the deck chairs, watching the sunrise creep up the Rockfish Valley and illuminate the Three Ridges Wilderness Area. Dogwood leaves glowed bright red, and the air smelled of fall—cool, crisp, and loamy. I thought I could see signs of tree foliage changing on the mountaintops along the Appalachian Trial—the AT, which coursed through the Blue Ridge Mountains on the western side of the valley.

I took a slow sip of coffee and sighed. "My father would have loved this. We climbed Mt. Katahdin, the terminus of the AT, many times. Years ago."

I'd thought our magical world would last forever because in my childish mind Daddy controlled both heaven and earth. Father Abraham was my guiding star. At the same time, I knew someday he wouldn't be there for me. Someday, I would have to find another guide. Someday, I would have to grow up and leave my family's home and all that entailed.

"Remember when you told me about your conversation with Gretchen when she was a teenager, about how she knew she couldn't stay with you forever?" I asked Keith.

"All children have to leave home someday."

"I think I learned that one night in 1969, six months before I left for college." Keith must have discerned the importance of what I was saying because he set his chess game aside and slid his chair closer.

"My father asked me to go for a walk after dinner. Mother probably put him up to it, knowing I'd need some fatherly send-off advice. Though March, the night was cold, more winter than spring, with fresh snow on the ground." I relived the scene in my head.

Daddy wore his wood-chopping jacket and cap with earflaps. I'd slipped on my parka and mittens Grammy had knitted for us. In moonlight, we hiked the neighborhood roads—Newton to Sanford to Seymour to Newton's entrance, looping back to our house.

"Along the way, as if out of nowhere, Daddy said in his deep bass voice, 'If you try to please everyone, Carole, you will fail.' His breath condensed into a cloud rising from the earth like an oracle's mist, but all I saw was fog. I felt ready for the physical leaving, but this was something else. Who do I need to please to succeed? I wondered. Instead of an answer, my mind whirled, and unfocused chatter came out of my mouth. 'Words, words, words!' My father scolded. 'Quiet yourself and think, Carole, think!'"

I shifted in the deck chair and looked across the valley. "My father's scolding is as clear to me today as it was back then." The memory made me doubly uncomfortable, because along with my inability to confront what my father had said, I'd revealed the scolding to Keith. In my mind, disapproval of my younger self equaled disapproval of me now, like the grasshopper incident and the overcooked eggs, problems I needed to work through but didn't know how, not yet.

I turned to face Keith. "Maybe he was trying to say something about himself or about me, and I babbled because I didn't want to hear it. Instead, I came away from the conversation vowing to succeed and earn Father Abraham's approval." I sighed again. "He was as close to a god as an atheist like me could get. And earning his love was my idea of heaven."

"All children deep down want their parents' approval," Keith said. "But when it comes time to leave home, some choose a different way of going about it. Before Gretchen left for college, I also took her for a walk after dinner one night. At the beginning of summer."

A new story and another connection. Now I leaned in and listened carefully.

"As we followed the sidewalks in the neighborhood, I told Gretchen that her behavior was disrupting everyone. She had to follow the house rules. No stealing, no drugs in the house, and no coming home drunk with strange men she wanted to sleep with. 'Clean up after yourself and keep regular hours,' I said. 'Be a good daughter and you will be welcomed back.'"

In my imagination, I saw them walking the neighborhood sidewalks as Heathcliff and I did. Keith had drawn the line with his daughter. Granted, he'd had to deal with a whole lot more than I did. But rule-enforcement was something I was not able to do, not consistently. Why not?

"Gretchen and I stopped in front of the townhouse, and I looked her in the face." He stared at me as if I was her. "I said, 'If you continue to misbehave and not participate in family life, we'll drop you at college, and no one will want to see you come back. Have a good life.'"

I stared back at him. "And what did she say?"

"She looked straight at me and said, 'Okay, I'll obey,' and she followed the house rules for the rest of the summer. But later she told me she couldn't wait to leave home. She said, 'Being free of your rules will be heaven.'"

I reached for our empty coffee cups. "Two heavens," I said. "Two perfectionists, two pursuits of happiness. Freedom and approval. Both tyrannies, both curses."

"True," Keith said and returned to his chess game.

For the rest of the day, whenever I gazed into Vanaprastha's sun-washed sky, I imagined shooting stars and time-lapsed star trails made invisible in daylight. Some truths can only be seen in darkness. I thought about Gretchen's curse, how she'd felt useless and wanted to die because she thought she was a failure. Her terrible curse had been mine, an invisible truth I could no longer deny. Except in college. My secret.

Go into the darkness, the Spirit said, *for there you will find light.*

Chapter 19

The Secret

We celebrated New Year's Eve in southern Virginia with Keith's dad. Early the next morning, Heathcliff and I walked under the black walnut trees behind Dad's big old house, which featured gingerbread trim and a wrap-around porch. Here Gretchen had spent summers and holidays, sleeping in the third-floor tower room. I gazed back at the house, imagining her climbing out the north window onto the roof to star-watch as Keith's youngest brother had.

The afternoon of New Year's Day, we swung by Vanaprastha to overnight before returning to Alexandria. Just before dawn, I dreamed of Gretchen again. This time she stood next to the futon, hovering close to me. I waited for her to speak.

"Lots and lots of work makes me happy," she said.

"Me too." I whispered, looking into her luminous face above me.

"And I can change my identity in a heartbeat to whatever I'd like without losing or gaining anything. What is identity? Who cares?"

I resisted the urge to chastise her flippancy.

She stared down at her hands. "Not working, though, made me feel useless and alone." I wanted to caress her arm. Alone. How did she know we shared that desperate feeling?

"I worked so I didn't wander the house feeling down, but I paid a high price." Like my father. I jolted awake, knowing what I had to do.

While driving north on 29 from Charlottesville toward Alexandria, I told Keith about Gretchen's visits to me in waking dreams. "She's spoken to me twice, using words from her journals." Keith shifted in his seat to look at me more closely.

"She visits me, too. She never says anything. I don't think she knows what to say. But she comes to comfort and sits quietly in my dreams." Not in mine, I thought. I told him about the "foil" dream and the "alone" dream I'd had that morning then took a deep breath.

"You know my father suffered with depression." I felt my eyebrows tensing up. "You also know I did, too—years ago." I stared at the road ahead, grateful to be driving a familiar route while forging into dangerously uncomfortable territory.

"There's something I haven't told you. I ran into some trouble during college."

"We all make adjustments when we leave home. Figuring out who we are, how to make a living, and who we'll walk through life with. It's not easy."

I sighed. "But I kept people at a distance and worked. More accurately, I stayed busy, so I wouldn't have time to think. I was afraid to find out who I was—I can see that now."

Work had kept me from wandering the house in a sick suit like my father, even before his sabbatical. Dear God, Keith doesn't know what he's married, I thought. I hate telling him this after all he's been through. But not telling the truth means I'm keeping secrets from him.

"Without God as my rock and foundation, I couldn't seem to leave home." I didn't dare look at him for fear he'd see my shame. "And I had a breakdown."

Keith didn't say anything. I had known this moment would come for months and had revisited that darkness many times to make sense of it. So, I took another deep breath and told him this story with as much honesty as I could.

At the beginning of my junior year at Wheaton College in Massachusetts, I'd set a goal to make top grades. My sister Jane had graduated with honors the previous spring, so I figured I'd shoot for that. I worshipped the god of numbers and measured my worth in grades. Immediately, trouble hounded me. I felt keyed up, and my moods swung wide. At night, I rolled from side-to-side for hours before falling asleep. The recurrent nightmare I'd had since childhood looped until I woke to failure yet again. I dragged around campus with a runny nose and headaches. Crumpled Kleenex littered my dorm room and stuffed my pants and jacket pockets. Every month, I suffered menstrual cramps as I had since the beginning in eighth grade. Now vomiting and diarrhea also plagued me unless I took the medication my mother's gynecologist had prescribed.

At the time, a mood-lifting drug called Daprisal was the favored medication to treat muscle pain for anything from athletic injuries to dysmenorrhea—menstrual cramps. Daprisal had unfortunate side effects. A few hours after taking a pill, I experienced a heightened sense of achievement, grandiosity, and obsessive thoughts. Then the euphoria broke, sending me crashing down into the depressing reality that I had accomplished nothing. Worse, I sensed life was nothing except less-than-satisfactory work and I was nothing. "You've done nothing, life is nothing, you're nothing," echoed in my drug-addled brain. To ride out the ups and downs, I lay in bed with a heating pad or locked myself in a practice room and played my flute for hours. Useless practice. After three or four days, I'd stop taking the pills and return to my normal routine with my mask of merriment in place—the show must go on. But in junior year, Daprisal offered less relief and more uncontrollable side effects.

That academic year, first semester exams moved from before Christmas to after. I studied through the holidays and returned to campus in early January. Bitter cold swept across New England with highs below freezing and lows in the teens, single digits, or below zero. The ducks on Peacock Pond swam in a huddled group to keep a section of water in the larger part of the pond open for feeding. Everyone came down with the flu or head colds. I was too stuffed up to sleep in the dorm's dry heat and too afraid to skip classes. So, I trudged across the bridge over Peacock Pond toward class in Mary Lyon Hall, huffing through my wool scarf.

One morning, a lone duck became ice-entombed in the smaller part of the pond near the bridge. I thought, I feel lousy, and that stupid duck is stuck again just like me. But as I approached Mary Lyon Hall, my thoughts echoed, "Poor ducky. We'll both be glad when this is over." At the same time, I knew that until we died, we'd both paddle, paddle, paddle, trying to keep the ice open, and every so often get stuck.

After slogging through a week of exams, I rested over the weekend and felt somewhat better when second semester classes began on Monday. Then in early February, first semester grades arrived. B's and a couple of A's. Not good enough, I told myself. My fault. I deserved it. I promised myself I would redirect, forge on, and try harder. In February's thaw, I donned boots like the lone duck's feet, paddled across campus, and waded into the library. I claimed a nesting spot in one of the remote study carrels. I'll do better next time, I assured myself.

Two weeks later, even though I'd taken the medication, I got stomach sick with my period. That evening, worn out yet keyed up, unable to rest, and battling the highs and lows of Daprisal, I came unraveled. The demon's poisonous voice screamed inside my head: "You're a fraud, and you know it. You're not smart. You're stupid, ugly, and fake." Blinding pressure built up then exploded. Tears, mucus, spittle, sweat, vomit, menstrual blood, and excrement drained out of me. My heart raced, and I shook uncontrollably. I struggled to fill my lungs with air. My brain ratcheted like a socket wrench tightening a bolt. Tighter, tighter, still tighter. My throat clenched, and utterances came out as high-pitched shrieks. I'd had episodes before but nothing like this.

I hid in my dorm room and phoned my father. For hours, I howled, sobbed, keened, and choked, about what I have no memory. My breakdown's self-absorption created a booze-like blackout for everything except the deafening ringing in my ears. I felt cracked open, totally exposed, and useless, as if I had no future except more of this. I wanted to die.

The next morning, I felt drained, neutered. Everything looked grey or beige. I sat in my beige dorm room, looking at a grey winter scene outside the grey window above my single bed. Even the neon pink bedspread looked beige. Symptoms lurked for days, so I avoided people as much as possible. I could barely move for fear of recurrence. My jaw popped whenever I opened my mouth. I didn't dare miss class but guarded my speech, fearing those uncontrollable, high-pitched shrieks. If others saw that shameful, out-of-control person, how would I ever recover? Or, more accurately, re-cover. The effort to control and hide my distress exhausted me.

I glanced at Keith. "I wrote to my parents, telling them I was scared to death of being alone. I wanted to be close to people and desperately wanted to be myself. What I didn't write was this: I was afraid my real self would be unacceptable and unworthy. Unlovable. At the same time, I mourned the loss of the messy, fearless, tree-climbing girl I felt I had to sacrifice on the altar of growing up. I thought perfectionism would help me find my way. Maybe if I stood perfectly on my own less-than-perfect feet, I'd feel okay about leaving Mother and my god, Father Abraham."

Keith remained silent for a long while, and I held my tongue, giving him time to process. As we drove along the Franconia-Springfield Parkway, about five miles from the townhouse, I broke the silence. "I didn't know what I was dealing with, Keith. I thought perfectionism was a good thing. I didn't realize it was a curse. Constant self-criticism and self-doubt, playing in my brain, and the blinding fear of failure. Horrible stuff. Horrible. Horrible."

Keith frowned. "But you don't have that now, right?"

"I've never been hospitalized or diagnosed, if that's what you're asking, and I haven't had an attack in years. After the breakdown, I stopped taking Daprisal, backed off my 'top grades' goal, and balanced my life better. My second semester grades improved."

He nodded. "Are you getting enough God time when you walk Heathcliff?" I heard his softness, which allowed me to stop worrying about myself.

"Yes, and our weight workouts help me blow off steam."

We pulled into the townhouse parking lot. Keith offered to unload the car and make supper while I took Heathcliff for his walk—we all needed to unwind after the drive.

As Heathcliff and I followed the sidewalk around each cul-de-sac, I remembered Mother accompanying me to an appointment she'd made with her gynecologist the summer before senior year of college. Her doctor recommended I take birth control pills to regulate my periods. The Pill was a Godsend for me—discomfort but no more missed days being sick every month and no more drug-addled mood swings.

Yet toward the end of summer, six months after my breakdown and with senior year approaching, I realized I was still the lone duck, swimming in the small section of the larger pond, thinking I possessed the power to succeed if only I paddled harder. More of the same, hoping for better results. Something was fundamentally wrong.

Heathcliff and I crossed the street at the end of the neighborhood and wound our way home. Suddenly, all the sound and imagery faded. I felt a gentle breeze. Calmness flowed over me, and a weight lifted.

I heard a voice—my voice—from all those years ago. *Help me because I don't know what else to do.* Gretchen's plea but my voice and directed toward... Oh. My. Goodness. I prayed to God that summer. I prayed to the God I didn't believe in. His grace gave me the ability to teach. And those quiet hums I felt throughout my career? Signs I was doing what the Spirit wanted me to do. The sound of God's love in me.

Out of darkness and into the light. "That's why student teaching went so well." I nearly shouted my indescribable joy.

During our supper of shrimp with cocktail sauce, cheese, baguette, olives, and salad, I told Keith what I'd remembered. "Isn't that amazing?" My eyes widened. "It's like removing a puzzle piece and discovering an entirely different picture underneath."

He smiled. "There's always another layer deeper in the onion. Keep going, Sweetheart."

"Oh, you taskmaster, just like our weight workouts."

"Grunt it up, old lady." Keith winked.

He knew I melted whenever he winked at me, and I knew how to volley. "I'll show you, old man." I glared at him across the table and grinned.

Our snorts of laughter rang throughout the house. In the living room, Heathcliff thumped his tail. I had told Keith the truth—discovered some, too—and we were laughing.

Freedom from fear brings indescribable joy, I thought, and freedom comes from God. This was my first inkling that my third stage of life reinvention might be about faith, about the "be." About identity.

Chapter 20

Mothers and Daughters

The situation in Connecticut was out of control. When Heathcliff and I visited Mother that winter, dirty dishes clogged the kitchen sink, food overflowed countertops, and packaging and products from mail-order catalogs surrounded her chair, spilling off the sofa onto the floor. I tidied as best I could. But when she sent me her Medicare bill with a penciled note asking, "What is this for," my sisters and I knew it was time for Mother to move. That spring, I put reinvention on hold and drove to Connecticut.

"So good to see you," I said, kissing her cheek. Food stains spotted her sweatshirt and pants. She attended to Heathcliff and ignored me.

I understood the slight. He was there to comfort. I had come to throw her life away.

My sisters and I had hoped to convince her to move three years earlier. She grudgingly filled out the application for an independent living community near me. "I'm fine right here," she'd said, patting the arm of her chair. Maintenance lapsed and accidents happened, fender-benders and face-first falls. I installed a medical alert system and insisted she wear the button.

When she finally gave into our pleas, saying, "I'll do it for you girls, so you don't worry about me," she chose to live near Jane and not me. Though I didn't ask her why she changed her mind—no point upsetting her further—Mother's choice hurt my pride. Did she have so little faith in me? At the same time, her decision wasn't a surprise. Mother had always shared her fears with Jane more than Leslie or me. In truth, Jane was better at dealing with Mother's anxiety than I was, though I didn't want to admit it. So, I ignored the thick stew of emotions simmering on my back burner and played to my strong suit: doing. In preparation for her move, I took the lead on first-round sorting of Mother's belongings.

For the next week, while Mother slept in bed or in her living room chair, I sorted. Keep. Pitch. Give away. Closets overflowed with holiday decorations; new toys for children already grown; sheets, towels, and blankets; clothing from the past thirty years, some soiled and worn, others in packages never opened; coins—collections of state quarters, Indian head nickels, colorized coin sets, silver bullion and gold Krugerrands hidden in file cabinets or behind books in bookcases; trinkets from mail-order catalogs under the beds, tucked into corners, and piled on every piece of furniture in the house.

"I want all of it," Mother had said whenever I mentioned sorting during previous visits—even bits of string squirreled in the corner of a kitchen drawer. "No, no, I want that," she'd said when I scooped them up. "My mother used to keep bits of string." In my zeal, I'd almost thrown out a cherished memory of her mother, my Grammy.

Now Mother didn't want any of it, not even the mail-order packages, which arrived almost daily. Silent in her chair, she stared off into space while Heathcliff nuzzled her.

The clutter exhausted her but energized me. Creating order gave me a sense of control. By eliminating the food rotting in her refrigerator and the stuff overflowing her closets, I thought I could stop Mother's deterioration, too, and retain our old mother-daughter relationship.

I found most of the jewelry and coins Mother had hidden and forgotten. "It will be a great treasure hunt for you girls," she'd said. "As my daughters, you'll be able to sniff them out." Money was no longer something made of nothing. The coins were real, and I couldn't wait to get rid of them. They gave intruders reason to break in—again. Why was she endangering herself and making it harder for her daughters? Was this her way of hanging onto us? Another ingredient in the pot of thick stew on my back burner that would have to wait.

On Wednesday morning, I asked Mother if she'd like to take lunch to Mrs. Taffel. "We could order take-out from The Gathering, for old times' sake."

Mother leaned forward. "Helen would like that. She has an aide staying with her now, since her last fall. They don't get out much."

WISDOM BUILDS HER HOUSE

"Then we'll order four meals and give her aide a break." I paused then sat on the corner of the sofa next to her chair. "Have you told Mrs. Taffel you're moving?"

Mother looked away. "I've been putting that off." She fingered the medical alert button suspended around her neck.

"The longer you wait, the harder it will be. And Mrs. Taffel will know you've known all along and chose not to tell her. That will hurt her feelings—maybe more than your leaving." I knew the move would be terribly hard for both of them. Mother and Mrs. Taffel had been best friends for almost sixty years.

Mother sighed and dropped her hand into her lap. "You're right."

"Tell her today, at lunch. I'll be right there. And we'll take Heathcliff."

I parked Mother's car in the Taffels' driveway and let Heathcliff out. We walked through the open garage, knocked on the door, and let ourselves into the house. In the kitchen, Mrs. Taffel sat at the head of the table. Her aide hovered near the counter.

"We brought lunch for everyone." I unpacked the to-go boxes and distributed them and drinks around the table.

The aide picked up her sandwich, chips, and coffee. "I think I'll go for a walk."

"Take your time," I said. "It's a nice day, and we'll be here for a while."

Heathcliff curled up between the two old friends who chatted through lunch. When she finished eating, Mrs. Taffel asked, "Would he like a bite of my sandwich?" Heathcliff's ears perked up.

"He'd love it," I said. "Make him sit for his treat."

Heathcliff moved close to Mrs. Taffel's chair and sat at her command. Unable to see him due to her blindness, she extended a piece of her sandwich in his direction. Heathcliff took the delicate morsel in his soft mouth then gulped.

"Good boy, Heathcliff, good boy," I said. "Now lie down."

We heard the door to the garage open. Mrs. Taffel's aide had returned.

"It's time for us to go." Mother pushed her chair away from the table.

I put my hand on Mother's arm so she would face me. "Tell her," I mouthed.

Mother's shoulders slumped. She turned to her friend. "Helen, I have something to tell you, and you're not going to like it."

"I think I know what it is, but go ahead."

"I'm moving."

"That's what I thought." I didn't see any reaction from Mrs. Taffel, but Heathcliff must have noticed something, because he got up and put his big head on her shoulder. She wrapped her arm around his neck and stroked his soft ear.

"When are you leaving?" Mrs. Taffel asked.

"In a month."

"So, you've known for a while."

"I didn't want to tell you." Mother's chin dropped to her chest.

"Well, it's a good decision for you, but not for everyone. I'm just fine right here." Mrs. Taffel patted the kitchen table.

"We'll come visit you, as often as we can while I'm here," I said.

On Saturday morning, Jessica arrived on the train from New York City, where she now lived and worked as a lawyer. "Of course, I'll come and help sort clothes," she'd said when I called to tell her what was happening. "It's Grandma, and we're family."

A wave of gratitude washed over me. "Thank you, Sweetheart, for taking time out of your busy schedule."

I picked her up outside the train station in New Haven. On the way home, we stopped at a local bistro for brunch. I filled her in on the task at hand.

"Every closet, Jessica, she's filled every single closet with clothes and stuff. Hers and your grandpa's, mine and Aunt Leslie's, the bathroom, girls' sitting room, hall, pantry, laundry, living room, and the cedar closet. I don't think she's gotten rid of anything since before Grandpa had his stroke in 1986."

At home, Jessica and I emptied one clothes closet at a time onto the living room floor. Mother stared blankly from her chair. Heathcliff had vacated the room, because there was no place for him to lie down for all the clothes.

"Tell me about this dress, Grandma." Jessica held up a pale lavender dress. "When did you wear this one?" My daughter's natural ease with her grandmother heartened me—for Mother's sake and mine. Maybe someday my daughter and I could have that ease between us.

Mother stared at the dress and shook her head. "Oh, Jessica, I don't remember." She had worn the lavender dress for Leslie's wedding.

"This turquoise outfit, isn't this the one you wore for your eightieth birthday party?"

Mother leaned forward. "I think you're right. You and David came, all the grandchildren, didn't you?"

"That's right," I said, happy she remembered the event and was showing some interest. Jessica and I hung the clothes that still fit in Mother's bedroom closet then tackled the bureau drawers in all the bedrooms. We threw stained or threadbare clothing into black garbage bags for trash pickup. The wearable went to Goodwill—two full carloads.

After we finished sorting clothes, Mother asked Jessica, "Is there any furniture you'd like to take?"

Jessica glanced around. "My apartment in the city is small, Grandma."

Mother persisted. "I'd like to think of you having something from the house, something from my past." To appease her, we walked from room to room.

In Mother's bedroom, Jessica spied Great Aunt Edna's cedar hope chest—compact, lightweight, and homemade. The chest, used to store linens and other practical items, had belonged to Grammy's sister. The two sisters, raised by their grandparents, had grown up poor. I thought about Grammy knitting socks and mittens for us and taking care of us after Mother was hurt.

Jessica turned to her grandmother. "I could put my photo albums and other memory stuff in that and store it in my closet."

I rubbed the palm of my hand over my heart. Instead of planning for and dreaming about the future, my daughter would shove reminders of her past into a hope chest and hide them in her closet, like me, hoping for a better past. I sighed an internal sigh. I couldn't fix this.

During Jessica's adolescence and early twenties, I had tried to help her sort out that past. For months after her father left when she was eleven, she struggled with anger and depression. Friendships were hard for her—maybe they are for everyone at that age. She resisted help. Although she excelled in school, Jessica sometimes made poor decisions as if seeking to fail.

"Maybe I just want to be an airhead," she'd said during her high school years.

"That's dangerous, Jessica," I said. "The world takes advantage of airheads."

There were car accidents and late nights, which turned into early mornings. Unlike my Father Abraham, her father wasn't waiting in the kitchen when she got home. Though I screamed and screeched, I never told her "Don't rebel" like my mother had. Maybe I should have, or maybe that would have made things worse for her. As a college freshman, she starved herself, and her boyfriends were just that. Boys. Had I been any different?

I shook my head, back to the present and the task at hand. After the three of us ate dinner at Teddy's, we dropped Mother at home and loaded Great Aunt Edna's hope chest into the car.

"Take Heathcliff with you," Mother said. "He'll keep you safe."

On the way to Manhattan, Jessica spoke about work and friends, though I sensed there were other things she wanted to say. I did my best to listen while attending to the road, avoiding wrong turns, and worrying about Mother. As we pulled up to the curb in front of the apartment building, Jessica's boyfriend came walking down the sidewalk. Her face showed surprise—he had not answered her texts.

My gut churned. Like her father, I thought, but I scolded myself. Mind your own business.

"Bye, Sweetheart," I said. "Let's visit at a less complicated time, okay?"

We hugged and kissed. She gave Heathcliff a pat goodbye. Then she and her boyfriend carried the hope chest into her apartment building.

On the drive back to Connecticut, I refocused on Mother. The next stage of her life—the fourth—meant a change in our relationship, a role reversal of sorts. There would be more changes in the next year, too. Later, I'd recognize these as stepstones guiding me toward the missing piece in my faith.

Chapter 21

Four Houses

Friday, June 29, 2012. Keith and I packed the Subaru mid-afternoon before the Fourth of July holiday and headed to Vanaprastha. During the drive, I reviewed my to-do lists for the three houses: Vanaprastha, Alexandria, and Connecticut, the latter now on the market. I had volunteered to handle the sale of Mother's house while Jane oversaw her move and adjustment to the new surroundings and living situations.

Arriving at sunset, Keith and I noted storm clouds to the west. Thunderheads billowed like colossal towers, rising into the sky behind the Blue Ridge Mountains. We watched through the three-story keyhole windows in the great room, captivated by the storm's updraft.

Suddenly, the storm broke and rushed down the Rockfish Valley. A wall of straight-line winds struck with unexpected force. Tall, deep-rooted poplars bowed in waves like a manic chorus line. Our house gulped then breathed in and out, gasping like some huge, living organism. We stood in awe—transfixed, powerless—and calm.

The storm's downdraft and straight-line winds passed as quickly as a tornado. Blue sky and late-day sunshine returned. Keith and I stared at one another. "Well," I said, searching for words, "that was interesting." Having shaken the earth, was God now appearing in roiling clouds and mighty winds? Was this another reminder about who's in control?

"Good thing we built the house to withstand hundred-mile-an-hour winds," Keith said.

Then the power went out. We heard our propane-fueled, whole-house backup generator sputter then roar. Electricity to the house was restored.

Internet news reported the storm, a Derecho, had cut a swath across Virginia, downing trees and powerlines. Our Alexandria neighbors reported no power loss, though outages were widespread across the area. Thankfully, neither of our homes sustained damage.

The backup generator hummed for days, keeping the house cool, food preserved, and water pumping. We checked on our neighbors and shared our resources—well water, hot showers, and freezer space. Keith and I felt blessed, well protected, and maybe a bit smug for having prepared. Vindication for past "unnecessary" precautions we'd taken.

Electrical power returned to the Rockfish Valley by the end of our week-long vacation. During the return trip to Alexandria, Keith spoke about interviewing for another work contract once the current one ended in two weeks. Unbeknownst to us, we'd have one more weekend to bask in the calm of Vanaprastha as a weekend retreat. Later, I'd view the Derecho as a warning sign for the whirlwind ahead.

The morning after we returned to Alexandria, after the last calm weekend at Vanaprastha, Keith's brother, who lived near their dad, phoned me.

"Dad's house is burning," he said. "Everyone's safe, no injuries."

Fire. Dad in southern Virginia. Another house.

I called Keith at work. "Dad's with his neighbor across the road." We all called him Dad, including me, because that's who he was. Not Father Abraham or Daddy. Just Dad.

The fire had started in an electrical outlet in the third-floor tower room where Gretchen had slept. "The first and second floors are mostly intact," I told Keith. "But there's smoke and water damage throughout the house." No discussion about what to do, just the facts.

"Okay, thanks for calling. We'll talk tonight." As the eldest of six and executor of his father's estate, Keith would be the one to oversee repair and renovation of Dad's house.

The following day, Keith announced his retirement. He worked to the end of the week and applied for accumulated paid vacation, which would run through mid-October.

At the time, the significance of these disasters—wind and fire only months after the earthquake—never crossed my mind. Although we'd foreseen our parents' shift into the fourth stage of life and had planned for our third stage retirement, the quick succession of events, and the "doing" that went with them, left us little time to ponder. Sometimes staying in the story is all God wants us to do.

I contacted our DC-area real estate agent and scheduled an appointment for him to view the townhouse. By the end of the week, we had our marching orders. Clear everything out of the finished part of the basement. Remove all personal items throughout the house. Leave furniture to show in the living room, dining room, and den. Keep the master bedroom intact. Move as much out of the other two bedrooms as possible.

For the next ten days, Keith and I loaded the Subaru and truck, drove both to Vanaprastha with Heathcliff, unloaded then drove back to Alexandria. Two weeks after Keith's last day at work, the Alexandria townhouse was on the market with late-October as our target closing date. During that time, we also made trips to southern Virginia. There, Keith coordinated with his siblings to oversee Dad's relocation and clear out his house.

Like Mother, Dad had amassed decades of stuff, so the fire was also a kind of blessing. But this time, I stood on the sidelines while Keith's family sorted and pitched damaged goods into a dumpster parked in the front yard. I saw myself as the newcomer, which I was, and Keith's supporter, the person who took orders and picked up lunch. But when Dad announced his decision to remain on the property in the "little house," a poorly maintained, vermin-infested outbuilding and, in my mind, far from safe, I shared my opinion with Keith then fumed in silence. I felt bereft and useless—powerless in the face of fire.

I sat in the driver's seat of the car, waiting for Keith, and stared at the useless hands in my lap. There was nothing I could do about Dad or my mother. Sadness, like billowing storm clouds I hadn't allowed myself to see, swelled in my chest. The turbulence of events so close together caused the two losses to collide. When the storm clouds collapsed, I wept for our parents and the changes that would be irrevocable for them. The third way doesn't always feel joyous or peaceful, I thought while lament poured down my face, tears I couldn't run from or fight.

In late July, my sisters and I accepted a contract on Mother's house. The real estate agent scheduled an inspection for August. Closing was projected for late September.

Four houses—Mother's, Dad's, the townhouse, and Vanaprastha—in four different directions. Two houses to sell, another to rebuild, and a home to settle into. All at once, we were confronted with all four stages of life: my childhood home where I'd spent my Brahmacharya student years, Keith's Grihastha householder home, Vanaprastha's third stage, and our parents' Sannyasa, the last stage. It was the strangest of strange times. And about to get stranger.

Inspection on Mother's house came back clean except for required radon treatment in the crawl space under the main part of the house. I signed a contract with a recommended company. Check. The next day, the agent did a routine tour of the house and discovered a leak in the oil tank in the garage and a puddle of water in the basement. She called a plumber, and I contacted Mother's fuel company and signed a contract for tank replacement. Check. Check.

The following day, the plumber gave us the bad news. Thieves had broken into the house and removed copper from the furnace room, from behind the washing machine in the kitchen extension, from the wing's basement under Mother's bathroom, and from the attic. The large copper pipes, connecting solar panels on the roof to a tank in the furnace room, were gone. Water had flooded the controller, sensors, and expansion tank, shorting out the electrical system. The house had no running water, heat, or air conditioning.

Earthquake, wind, fire, now flood. In a season like this, all we can do is keep doing. This time, instead of complaining, I prayed, listened, and with Keith designed a plan of action.

After Labor Day, we packed the Subaru with ten-gallon jerry cans filled with water for washing and self-flushing the one useable toilet, drinking water, aerobed, sleeping bag, TV tables, folding chairs, dog bed, laptop, a mobile access point, and books, including Gretchen's journals. Heathcliff and I headed north to Mother's house while Keith headquartered at Vanaprastha to tend the other three houses.

In Connecticut, I unpacked the car, plugged in the microwave, and placed Heathcliff's food and water bowls on the kitchen floor. Two TV-tables made an L-shaped desk in the corner of the dining room where the toybox and blackboard used to be. I set up our beds in the girls' sitting room, which connected the main house to the bedroom wing.

The next morning, sitting on the front steps of Mother's empty house, I paged through one of Gretchen's journals while waiting for the plumber and keeping an eye on Heathcliff, who frolicked across the lawn. I realized that selling my mother's house was part of another ending. Forty years ago, I had left home. Now my childhood home was leaving me.

I wanted to pity myself, of course. Then the Indian summer sun cast rays of light across the yard. A gentle breeze rustled the leaves, and a red-tailed hawk called to her offspring. I remembered harvesting end-of-the-season vegetables from the garden, winter sledding and ice skating, summer swims in the pool with my sisters, our three beds lined up like piano keys.

Thank you for this wonderful place and for the people who lived here, I prayed, *and for having been able to share this home with my children.*

A school bus chugged along Newton Road, and grasshoppers jumped in the overgrown field in front of the house. "Thank you for the hard lessons, too," I said out loud to God. "They shaped me into who I am."

The plumber drove his truck up the driveway and parked in the turnaround. Heathcliff barked, hackles up. "Here, boy, it's okay." I leashed Heathcliff and met the plumber at the breezeway door.

"Thank you for coming," I said. "I'm afraid there's a lot to reconnect."

"Let's have a look." He stepped into the breezeway and headed to the furnace room.

I sighed with gratitude. This will be an excellent goodbye. And another stepstone.

Chapter 22

Mistakes Were Made

One morning when the plumber was on another job and no other house repairs were scheduled, Heathcliff and I picked up lunch at The Gathering and went to see Mrs. Taffel. Now that her aide had been reassigned, Mrs. Taffel lived alone with assistance from a woman who'd helped Mother toward the end of her time in Connecticut. I knocked on Mrs. Taffel's door, announced myself, and walked in with Heathcliff's nose following the lunch bag.

"We thought you might enjoy some company."

"Come in, sit down. I'll get plates. What would you like to drink?"

"Water's fine." I was amazed how she navigated, given her blindness. After fifty years in her house, I guessed she knew where everything was.

Heathcliff bellied down beside Mrs. Taffel's chair. Waiting.

We chatted about our families, catching up on the news. As lunch wound down, she tore off a piece of her sandwich. "Sit," she said to Heathcliff. After giving him the morsel, she cupped both hands around his big head and caressed his soft ears.

"Oh, how I'd love to have another dog."

"I remember Jetty and Silver." Jetty was the Taffel's black lab when I was a child and Silver their German shepherd. "During the summer, Jetty made the rounds of neighborhood families who ate dinner outside when the weather was nice. He used to come to our house, put his chin on the picnic table, and wait."

Mrs. Taffel smiled. "Everyone loved Jetty, and he loved children."

"But you had to watch his tail. He could wipe out the little ones with that tail." We both laughed. "And he had a way of charming us out of our ice cream cones, too." I picked up our plates and glasses and took them to the sink. "I don't remember Silver coming over unless all of you came."

"Silver was protective and got into fights with other dogs, especially males. Except for Jetty. Jetty never met a stranger. Silver... I was glad to have him watch over my children."

As he did the day of Mother's "accident."

I could have asked Mrs. Taffel what happened but didn't. Maybe that was a mistake. But I thought if there was ever a good time to ask, this was not it. She had almost lost her best friend in 1957, and now her best friend had left. I shoved the past back into my brain's memory closet.

While reading Gretchen's journals at Mother's house, I thought about my own daughter. What had Jessica wanted to say to me when she came to help sort back in May? In August, before I left for Connecticut, she'd sent me a copy of Jonathan Franzen's *Freedom*. This wasn't the first time Jessica had communicated with me through media. During her early college years, she'd asked me to see *Anywhere but Here*, starring Susan Sarandon as an impulsive, brash mess of a single parent and Natalie Portman as her practical, academically talented daughter. As I recall, our discussion about the movie was not illuminating. Although I could see aspects of Jessica in the daughter, I couldn't see anything of myself in Susan Sarandon's character. I wasn't ready to view myself as a single mother who made an idol of her children and looked to her daughter for redemption. Maybe that's what Jessica wanted me to understand, maybe it wasn't. I never asked.

When Jessica sent Franzen's novel, I had a better sense of what she might be telling me: that I needed to let her live her own life—as Natalie Portman's character needed her mother to do—and keep my opinions about her personal life to myself. But I had the same problem with Franzen's novel as I did with the movie: not much in the book seemed like me. Many of Franzen's characters enjoyed "freedom" without striking out on their own and deemed themselves entitled to others' money. Also, most of the major characters were unfaithful in marriage. And although Franzen mixed Judaism and Christianity with liberal and conservative politics, there was a striking lack of spiritual depth in all his characters.

The thought occurred to me that using media to communicate was like writing letters instead of journal entries or speaking face-to-face. One step removed. Less honest. Without thinking about how this might play out, I decided to close the distance when we next saw each other.

We kept in email touch and made a date for her to visit while I was in Connecticut.

She arrived one Saturday morning on the train. After lunch, we took a walk. The late summer sun and a light breeze caressed us as we ambled across the Russells' big lawn. I let Heathcliff off leash so he could roam our old stomping grounds.

"What did you want me to understand about Franzen's *Freedom*?" I asked.

"Patty," she said then added, "You can be mean, like Patty." I glanced at my daughter. Her arms, which had swung free, now stilled.

In *Freedom*, Patty was the mom, the mostly good person who baked cookies for her community and, like me, had a daughter and son. She could also be unkind in her frankness and frustration with life, placing high expectations on herself and berating herself for mistakes. In the book, Patty titled her autobiography, *Mistakes Were Made*. Ironically, Jessica also was the name of Patty's oldest child. Had Patty placed high expectations on her children, as I had, and equated meanness with strength as the puppy-slapping boy had? As I had?

I looked at my thirty-two-year-old daughter. Her curly blonde hair was spiked short and dyed flame red. I wondered what her bosses might think about her appearance.

"Thank you for telling me this. I'm sure it wasn't easy." I paused to gather my thoughts. "I knew you were having a hard time growing up. I didn't know how to help."

We walked in step, more gauged than earlier.

"And yes, I was prideful." I waited for some reaction to my confession. When she remained silent, I thought I'd miscalculated my share of the blame, expecting her to own up to her share—as I measured it. So, I offered more truth. "I'd already failed as a wife. I didn't want to fail as a mother, too."

By connecting wife-failure with fear of mother-failure, I realized I had, indeed, expected Jessica to redeem me, like Susan Sarandon's movie character. But unlike Natalie Portman's character, Jessica had not. Her prodigal past flashed into my mind. A past I resented, a past I wanted her to apologize for, a past I didn't know how to forgive.

I'd been at my wit's end, exhausted from her vampire hours. Rowing our family boat as a single parent felt like paddling upstream against a strong current of "anything goes" popular culture and her father's "anything goes" drinking and infidelity. When Jessica's I-can-do-anything-I-want behavior resulted in frightening car accidents and other scrapes, I rose to save her again and again. I didn't want to believe she would tell me whatever she thought I wanted to hear in order to get her way. My dear friend and colleague recognized the straits I was in and recommended Al-Anon, a support group for people affected by others' addictive behavior like my ex-husband's.

Al-Anon. For enablers like me who think they are in control and can keep bad things from happening. Who obsess over busyness and checklists. Who think they can protect others from poor decisions by screaming and scolding them into goodness—then bail them out. For mothers like me who know they need to draw the line yet continue to rescue their children because of fear they might lose them.

I attended my first Al-Anon meeting one summer evening in Texas. Passing among the smokers gathered in the parking lot behind a two-story strip-shopping center, I held my breath. After ascending the stairs, I bypassed the AA room and stepped into Al-Anon.

We sat on metal folding chairs around a laminate folding table and introduced ourselves in turn. Everyone said how grateful he or she was to be there. I didn't follow the rules.

"My name is Carole." I felt anger rise from my gut into my throat.

"Hi, Carole," everyone chorused.

"I'm happy you're glad to be here, but I'm not." I thrust my chin into the air. "I came here to get some advice about how to fix the people who are causing this chaos in my life."

Silence. I glanced around the table and saw slow smiles and heads nodding.

After a long pause, I bowed my head. "So, I guess I need to be here."

Al-Anon was the opposite of fixing. People listened to one another and gave suggestions. Nobody told anyone what to do. How people managed the vicissitudes of life fascinated me. They spoke calmly about choosing not to bail out family members, who were in desperate trouble. Instead, they chose to provide information and not support dysfunctional behavior or take responsibility for others' actions. Detach with love. Let go and let God.

In time, I breathed easier as I crossed the parking lot and ascended the stairs. I looked forward to Al-Anon meetings. The stories encompassed every demographic, like variations on similar themes. While listening, I nodded my head, seeing the slivers in others' eyes. I learned some strategies for staying calm and imagined myself inching up the

Twelve Steps. The veterans knew I was missing the big log in my own eye. They encouraged me to attend the Sunday evening meetings when AA and Al-Anon met together.

I had to force myself to go and listen to stories of addiction: sex, drugs, alcohol—and shopping. I didn't want to admit my own addiction to control. There wasn't much I could do about my ex-husband, but I wanted Jessica to follow the rules and stop worrying me. I wanted her to change, not me. I wanted them all to change. But they didn't. So, I ran away as fast as I could, and that was the end of Al-Anon for me. Maybe that was a mistake.

Heathcliff loped across the Russells' big lawn toward Jessica and me, grinning and snorting his pleasure. In contrast, Jessica maintained her silence. I would have done better if I'd kept my mouth shut. But my tit-for-tat need for her to confess her past sins—maybe even express some gratitude for my rescues—overruled the lessons of Al-Anon. If not a full pound of flesh, I wanted at least an ounce. And I was willing to run over her to get what I wanted.

"Sometimes you frightened me with the things you did." Exasperation claimed my voice. "It got to the point where I didn't want to answer the phone. I was so afraid of losing you. Why all the partying and car accidents? What was going on?"

"I don't know, Mom." The voice of a lonely child of divorce, not the accomplished professional woman she'd become.

"Have you prayed about that?"

Her eyes narrowed. "I don't do that." She didn't want to know the Father who waited for her to come home.

An impenetrable wall rose between us. *Lord, help me, I'm making a mess.*

As we followed the path from lawn to woods, across the stream, and up the gentle slope to Mother's house, I tried again. "There are things in me I'm trying to change. All my life, I've tried to do good. But I make mistakes, sometimes the same ones over and over, and I'm trying to figure out why." My words sounded weak, but they were the best I could do at the time.

I stopped and placed my hand on her arm. "I'm sorry, Sweetheart, I could not always be who you needed me to be. I tried to be both parents. But I'm a lousy father and sometimes not a great mother either." And I am not God.

Jessica touched my hand. "That's okay, Mom."

But I knew it wasn't, not for either of us. Why hadn't I kept my mouth shut? And why hadn't she confessed and thanked me as I wanted her to?

Back at the house, we noticed water leaking into the breezeway from under the furnace room door. One of the new solder joints had given way. The flood had returned. We turned off the water and mopped up the mess.

That evening, at the New Haven train station, I pulled the car into a drop-off parking space. "Thanks for coming." I caressed Jessica's arm, and Heathcliff nuzzled her.

"Sure, Mom. Be safe. I don't want anything to happen to you."

"Oh, Jessica, I'm fine. Heathcliff's a terrific guard dog." I remembered my mother, saying he'd keep me safe the night I drove Jessica back to New York with the hope chest.

"I love you, Sweetheart." We kissed goodbye.

"Love you, too." She hopped out of the car.

I watched my daughter disappear into the train station. *Freedom, Al-Anon, Jessica, Gretchen—what are the connections?* I asked. *Lord, help me, why do I keep making mistakes? I get close to the third way with Jessica then bail. Why this stumbling block?*

Heathcliff rested his chin on my shoulder, and I stroked his ears like Mrs. Taffel had. We listened for a few moments. But this time there was no reply.

"I guess that still means wait," I said. "And you and I are not good at waiting."

Chapter 23

Freya Joins the Pack

Toward the end of my Connecticut house stay, Keith called, which was unusual since we communicated via email rather than phone. I was sitting on the front stoop again, watching Heathcliff frolic in the late afternoon sun. Keith said he was at Vanaprastha. But not alone.

"I did a bad thing." He sounded remorseful. Sort of.

"Yes." I adjusted the phone so I could hear better.

"I adopted a dog."

Keith and I had talked about getting a buddy for Heathcliff to play with once we retired to Vanaprastha. Before I left for Connecticut, we picked up a flyer from Almost Home volunteers, staffing the SPCA booth at our local Farmers Market. The flyer's picture showed a good-sized shepherd-mix with one flopped ear. Keith studied the photograph, read her profile, and tucked the flyer in his back pocket.

"The shepherd-mix?" I smiled into the phone.

"That's the one."

I chuckled. "I figured you might get lonely and go see her."

According to the staff at Almost Home, she disliked female dogs but got along well with males who enjoyed playing rough like Heathcliff. She and her brother had been feral before they landed in the shelter. Her brother was out for adoption, but she'd been in the shelter for a while. Failed adoptions and her reputation for being snippy hurt her chances for home placement.

Snippy, I thought. Dislikes females. Would she like me? I wasn't thinking about whether I'd like her yet, or that maybe we shared those qualities.

"They wanted to see how I handled her," Keith said. "She obeyed me on leash. So, I squatted, looked in her eyes, and asked if she wanted to be our dog."

"And?"

"She jumped into the front seat of the truck." With his assistance, he later confessed.

She was adjusting well to the mountain house, Keith told me, and smelled Heathcliff so she knew there was another dog around somewhere. When he let her off leash, she'd stayed close and came right back when he called.

"She's very smart. Last night I was watching TV in the basement and eating a bagel with cream cheese. I asked if she wanted the last piece, and she sat for it. When she sat for more, I said, 'No more, no more bagel. That's all there is.'"

He laughed. "She studied my face then went upstairs to the kitchen." I imagined the click-click of her toenails on the stairs and tile floor. "She came back down, holding the bagel bag in her mouth, and presented it to me, no bite marks on bag or bagel. I guess she wanted to show me that I was mistaken—there were more bagels." Now he chuckled. "I hadn't caught her in the act, so I could hardly chastise her for getting up on the kitchen counter."

"And you toasted another bagel." I was totally charmed by this smart girl.

"Well, I sort of had to." He laughed again.

"Is she healthy?"

"Yes, but she has a golf ball-sized cyst on her head and extra toes on both back feet. They're non-functional, rather ugly. I'm concerned they might snag when she runs in the woods."

I nodded into the phone. "The vet can take care of those things. Anything else?"

"She's active and alert and has some fears: open spaces, closed spaces. Whenever I give hand signals, commands, or correction, she ducks her head, trembles, and pees on the floor."

Poor girl, she's been abused and needs a home. I remembered Heathcliff's fears and months of stress-related messes. Together, Keith and I could handle the adjustment.

"What's her name?" I asked.

"I call her Freya." The goddess of women, beauty, love, war, and magic.

I thought of our two daughters, Keith's and mine. "I can't wait to see her."

After we hung up, I began to worry. Would I be able to handle another dog, an adult female? I still struggled with Heathcliff, who despite training behaved like a big, adorable, stubborn, sensitive, goofy adolescent pup. Would I be able to love her as much as him?

One evening during my last week in Connecticut, Mrs. Taffel invited me to dinner. This time, I left Heathcliff at Mother's house to guard the new repairs. The woman who helped Mrs. Taffel cooked a meal of chicken breasts, mashed potatoes, green beans, and cake.

Another excellent goodbye.

For the rest of our stay, Heathcliff and I didn't leave the house and surrounding grounds, other than driving to the grocery store or Mrs. Taffel's or the Woodbridge Town Hall to pick up building permits and a copy of the police report for Mother's insurance claim. While at the police station, I thought about asking for records from 1957. But I didn't. The Spirit had more stepstones for me to cross before I was ready to seek the truth and reveal my secret. My real secret.

A few days after our phone conversation, Keith called again. "I invited our neighbor for dinner last night. I wasn't paying attention and missed the signs. Freya snapped at him when he walked into the house."

"Is he all right?" Visions of worst-case scenarios flew across my brain.

"Yeah. I feel bad about what happened."

"Feeling bad doesn't protect visitors or Freya." My gut leaped at the chance to dispense some tit-for-tat feedback. "I know you love her, but you trust her too much. Please don't put her in these situations, not till we know how she's going to react. She trusts you to help and protect her. We've got to teach her how to greet our visitors without snapping. Otherwise, we won't be able to keep her."

"I know. You're right. I'll be more vigilant. We'll work on this together when you and Heathcliff get home." We talked another minute then hung up.

Okay, I thought, he took that well. Even though I'd sort of snapped at him.

I wasn't proud of myself for blaming Keith and dishing out a lecture. I'd offered more grace to the puppy-slapping boy. But I excused my behavior because I was worried about Freya's. Her snippiness was a dangerous stumbling block. Didn't I have enough to deal with?

And as with Al-Anon, I wanted her to change, not me.

We closed on Mother's house in Connecticut at the end of September. Other than "mission accomplished" relief, feelings about this ending got pushed aside like mementos tossed into a large moving box marked, "To be sorted." As soon as the attorney called, confirming all paperwork was in order, I packed the Subaru, locked the house, dropped the keys at the real estate office, and headed south on 95 with Heathcliff. We spent the night at the townhouse in Alexandria and the next day drove to Vanaprastha.

I pulled the Subaru into the garage and opened the back. Heathcliff jumped out, peed in his favorite spot next to the woodpile, then raced up the deck stairs with me right behind him. Freya stood between us and Keith.

Both dogs tensed and low growled, hackles up. Their bodies jerked and postured—Heathcliff defending me, Freya defending Keith. As they sniffed nose-to-nose and noses-to-tails, I side-stepped around them and gave Keith a hug and kiss. The dogs settled.

I retrieved their food bowls and filled them with kibble. "Heathcliff, Freya, dinner." I held the bowls over their noses. They followed me across the deck to their water bowl outside the kitchen door. Both sat and waited for my signal. Watching the two of them, eating side-by-side, I was reminded of the Taffels' Jetty and Silver, the black lab and the shepherd.

That evening, our dogs played bitey-face, rolling and racing across the deck. Keith and I nodded to one another. Now we were a pack of four.

Maybe.

In the days that followed, I walked, fed, and groomed both Heathcliff and Freya. She had the beautiful color and markings of a German shepherd and the strong body and wide hips of something big. Though she out-smarted Heathcliff—tricking him into leaving his favorite bed then lying there looking smug—she was submissive, especially about food. She stood behind him at mealtime and held back, squinting her eyes to avoid being whacked by his tail as he ate.

I advocated for her, not allowing Heathcliff to bully her out of her share. But Freya didn't reward me for any of my efforts to befriend her. She sat beside Keith during the day, slept on the floor on his side of the bed at night, and rolled belly-up for pets from him every morning. Her big brown eyes gazed at him with adoration. We called this expression her Princess Di look: head down, eyes up.

Keith was her savior. Not me. He rescued her. Not me. She trusted him. Not me.

Would she come to trust me as Heathcliff did and seek my affection? Was I jealous of Keith's relationship with Freya? Did he love her more than me?

Bah. I was back where I started with Gretchen. Would I ever be able to get passed this stumbling block? Later, I would come to understand that stumbling blocks are God's stepstones.

In early October, we received a serious offer on the townhouse and moved most of our remaining belongings to the mountain house. Keith with Freya stayed at Vanaprastha and watched over his dad in southern Virginia while I drove with Heathcliff to Alexandria to handle inspection repairs and those due to vandalism. Thank goodness the damage was small compared to the flood in Connecticut: two fence posts, snapped off at ground-level, soon replaced. Heathcliff and I rode out Hurricane Sandy in late October. The following morning, right after I'd cleaned up yard debris, the buyer's real estate agent arrived to take pictures, confirming the ready-for-closing condition of the house.

On Halloween, Heathcliff and I handed out candy to the neighborhood kids and said goodbye. Keith and Freya arrived the next day. The two dogs frolicked on the playground like best buddies happy to be together again. All of us slept in the master bedroom, Keith and I on the aerobed, the dogs on their dog beds. Early the next morning, we loaded the dogs into the Subaru and our belongings into the truck and drove both vehicles to the attorney's office for closing. Another mission accomplished, another ending with feelings boxed and set aside for sorting.

Four, three, now two houses. For six months, we'd stayed in the story, doing what needed to be done. We felt like running a victory lap. Yet, I knew the past that had happened in the houses we'd sold—Gretchen's home and mine—was not behind us but ahead, and the truth would not wait forever.

Chapter 24

Unsettled

Boxes huddled in corners of the house and cluttered the garage. Five months had passed since our move to Vanaprastha. Relaxing in his new freedom, Keith didn't seem pressed to do anything right away. But I felt unsettled, unable to look back or move forward.

One morning after breakfast, I took a chance and asked, "Could we put pictures on the walls today? It won't take long."

"Sure, we could do that."

I popped out of my chair and headed to the garage for a stepladder. Back in the great room, I said, "If it's okay with you, I'd like to put Gretchen's charcoal drawing in the triangle gable above the dining room table." The picture was a still-life drawing of two candles, a peck basket of fruit, and a wine glass sitting on a table. A cute mouse—ears back, eyes scanning, nose sniffing—perched next to the wine glass.

"I don't want any memorials to Gretchen," Keith had said the day I found her portfolio and asked about her artwork. "She wouldn't have wanted that either." I only framed the pictures he liked, the ones he thought were among her best work: still-life and portraiture.

For the wall at the top of the loft stairs, he chose the picture that had hung in our bedroom in Alexandria. The last picture Gretchen drew for him. He told me he'd asked her to draw carnations, his favorite flower, and she drew thorny roses.

I studied Gretchen's drawing and smiled. Prickly and contrary. Like her father.

"They're pretty flowers," I said. "And you'll see them whenever you come upstairs to your writing loft." We had built the mountain house, as he'd written in his online letter, and now he was writing his father's World War II stories, and others.

For the guest bedroom, we selected photographs of our four children—Gretchen, Alex, Jessica, and David—and Gretchen's colored anime, a group portrait of the employees of the art supply store where she'd worked during college.

"Gretchen got into anime and was quite good," Keith said. I heard both discernment and pride in his voice. In front to the far left in the picture, Gretchen sat cross-legged on the floor. Her right hand posed behind her head, and her left hand gestured a peace sign. She winked one big anime eye and playfully stuck out her tongue.

Keith and I stepped back to gaze upon our display of pictures. "Children are blessings given to us for a short period of time," he said, "then we have to let them go to live their own lives." We stood in silence for a while, looking at our blessings.

I saw Keith straighten and tense. "She used herself up, burned herself out." No nuance, just the facts. "I told her that's what she was doing. She did it anyway. Then she asked, 'Why is this happening to me?' She knew why but didn't want to give up control."

By then I'd learned more about the troubles in Gretchen's life that had led Keith to say "Yes. I know. I lived it." He knew Gretchen would not have been blessed with her own children. The year before her death, treatment for genital viruses left her sterile. She suffered another outbreak a few months before she died. Perhaps worse, I'd reached the point in her journals where she stopped telling herself the truth. She spun magical tales of wishful thinking about love and wove them into thoughts about her future and death. *If you tell the truth, you're dead*, she'd written in 1996. Five years later, toward the end of her life, the consequence of truth-telling had reversed: *If you don't, you're dead.*

While carrying the stepladder down the stairs, I recalled what Gretchen had written in an earlier entry: "I want distance, I want to have that and call it love." Safe distance and love. Our attempts to have both at the same time crippled us with ambivalence. She suffered terrible consequences, and so had I when hitting the "why is this happening to me" failure of my first marriage. When I suffered that major defeat and shocking humiliation, when I deprived myself of food and sleep, and when the sun rose in psychedelic colors.

I remembered that morning from twenty years ago like it was yesterday. The morning I knew I would die and leave my children motherless if I didn't change. The morning I knew I would have to let go in order to live. The morning I surrendered and immediately sensed a mysterious Spirit, peaceful and authentic. The blessing of children and letting go—there my path and Gretchen's diverged.

At Vanaprastha, I returned the stepladder to the garage. I hadn't consulted God about marrying my first husband. Even if I had, that didn't mean things would have gone well—for Gretchen either. Different choices would have resulted in different consequences, not necessarily better or worse. We are not in control. Not my script or will but Thine, though God's plan is often a mystery. On rare occasions, I glimpsed why Thy will be done might be happening. Most often I didn't, or maybe after the fact. For instance, the irony of settling in while thinking about letting go—the same as preparing for a hurricane while reading *Falling Upward*—was completely lost on me. Maybe because letting go meant loss of control.

Thy will be done. Then we have to let our loved ones go. Except.

Each day that spring, we observed nature's greening creep from the Rockfish Valley up the Blue Ridge Mountains and anticipated another change of season: a letting go that was expected yet an unwelcome stepstone for both of us. As work on Dad's house neared completion—Keith had managed most of the renovations—his eighty-nine-year-old father's health was failing. We made frequent trips to see Dad in the hospital and rehab—more often in the hospital. The last time Keith visited, Dad told him he didn't think he'd leave the hospital again. Thereafter, Keith carried his cellphone in his pocket.

Sunday, April 21, 2013. A clear day, a bit chilly though warm in the sun. After church, Keith and I ate brunch at one of the local restaurants. As we walked to our car in the parking lot, Keith's cellphone rang—his father's doctor calling from the hospital.

Dad was losing his fight against infection. They'd exhausted every medication and non-surgical treatment at their disposal and would have to operate in order to find out where and what the infection was. But Dad was too weak to survive an operation.

"I understand," Keith said. "I give my permission not to treat. Do you need me to sign papers to that effect?" My discerning husband. Calm in crises. Experienced with loss.

"Well, this is it," Keith said after the call ended. He stood in the middle of the parking lot. Holding his phone face up. Staring at the ground. Not moving.

Faith would not spare him from grief any more than when he lost his darling daughter. Keith and Dad were buddies. This time, my husband was losing his buddy.

Dad. Upbeat, kind, generous, the man who gave us bear hugs when we visited, including me the first time we met during his 60th wedding anniversary celebration. Dad. A genuine, loving person, one of the best I'd ever known.

I took Keith's strong left hand in my strong right. We walked to our car, side-by-side, our bookends leaning inward. Then I drove us home.

Dad's big generous heart gave out four days later. Though he'd never live in his refurbished house, he would dwell with the Lord forever. "Everyone has only so much time on earth," Keith often said. "Time is the most valuable thing we have."

Thy will be done. Then we have to let people go. Except.

My mother had not wanted us to attend funerals. Too morbid, she said, best to focus on life and living. We didn't have a funeral for my father, just a viewing and burial, then later a memorial service at the university. Nothing religious, of course. Thus, I had little knowledge of church protocols, none in a front-row setting except for Keith's mom's service in 2006, a few months before we married. Seated between Dad and Keith, I watched what everyone else did and followed suit. Except for crying. Not in public, that is.

Keith's family scheduled Dad's visitation at the funeral home for the first of May, a Wednesday evening, and the memorial service the following morning at St. John's Lutheran Church in Farmville. Full honors' burial at Arlington National Cemetery would take place at a later date. I handled the practicalities for our trip to Farmville: booking a motel room, washing and ironing clothes, withdrawing extra cash, and making kennel reservations. That I could do.

Thus far on my journey, I'd followed the Spirit's guidance, even the unsettling "Excepts." Now, a stepstone appeared where I refused to place my feet. The Spirit guided me there anyway.

Chapter 25

Untrusting

The day before Dad's viewing was overcast yet pleasant with highs in the 60s. Mid-morning, I let the dogs out to run the mountain. They usually ran for thirty minutes, maybe an hour, two at the most. But after two hours passed, I began to worry. And the longer they were gone, the more I blamed Freya.

We called her our Iditarod dog for her wolfie looks and love of snow. During warm months, she cooled herself in the streams that fed Reid's Creek, which flowed into the Rockfish River, and came home covered with mud, muzzle to tail. Heathcliff, though a lab with webbed feet, disliked getting wet and stayed clean, unless he found something smelly to roll his ruff in, turkey poop being his favorite. Same with Freya or worse, skunk.

Because of her feral history and pack loyalty, she brought home critters—squirrels, turkey chicks—or bones she'd found, once a small deer head, freshly killed. Having a strong aversion to dead animals, I called Keith whenever Freya dropped a trophy on the deck.

"Your dog is home, and she has something for you," I'd say.

She and I had developed a routine for hosing off after her muddy escapades. "Freya, come," I'd say, and she'd dutifully follow me to the back terrace. She stood while I hosed one side and raised her back leg so I could reach under her belly. "Turn," I'd say, and she'd oblige then raise the other back leg. After a couple of hosing-offs, I didn't have to say anything—she knew the drill.

I anticipated another hosing session with Freya when the dogs returned. But minutes ticked by with no sign of either of them. I walked outside of the house, calling and blowing the dog whistle. Two hours grew to three. I paced between the kitchen and living room, as I had the night Jessica ran away and the day the earthquake hit.

"The dogs have never been gone this long," I said out loud. Keith was in the loft, engrossed in writing his science fiction novel and probably didn't hear me. "I'm worried something's happened." Keith didn't answer. At this point, I didn't expect him to.

I'd told Keith I hadn't had a panic attack in years, so I tried not to get too close to the edge where the poisonous demon lurked, something I'd learned after my breakdown in college and again after my first husband left. But I didn't have control over the outcome of this situation any more than the morning Heathcliff disappeared in the dark, chasing a squirrel.

Three hours, then four. I jumped into the car and drove up and down the mountain road with the windows open, calling the dogs' names. My heart pounded. At home, I paced. Windows, clock, doors, deck. Windows, clock, doors, deck. I pinched my face and plucked at my clothes. *No, no, no, not this, not this.*

"What if they don't come home?" I asked Keith. My frantic pitch must have caught his attention. He pushed his chair back from his desk and leaned over the loft railing.

"Either they'll come home, or they won't." ENTJ. Totally logical. And the wrong answer.

"That's not what I want to hear." I flapped my right hand back and forth, batting his words away. My neck craned and ached from looking up.

I took a shallow breath. "I want you to tell me they'll come home." My voice wavered. "I'm worried, and I want you to worry, too."

"You want me to worry." Keith stood still and spoke calmly. Calm in crisis.

"Yes. I mean, no." I stepped back to see Keith better and ease the crick in my neck. If he lost it then I'd have to hold it together. At least one of us had to stay calm, and both would be better.

Without saying another word, Keith returned to his desk. He had said what I needed but didn't want to hear: he wasn't God, and neither was I. Thy will be done. Then we must let them go. Trust, no matter what happens.

I stood in the middle of the great room and prayed inside my head. Fighting words. *Are you asking me to give up Heathcliff and Freya? I've already given up my career, and now I'm trying to do what you want me to do. What more do you want me to give up? Our children? Our house? My husband?*

Keith. Oh, dear God, did I hear what I was saying? Here he'd lost Dad and might lose two more buddies, and I was spewing worry all over him. This was a trust test, and I was failing. I opened the palms of my hands. *Forgive me, Lord, I'll try to do better.*

I sat down, picked up a book, and pretended to read. I curbed my pacing to once every ten minutes and looks out the window to occasional glances. When tempted to blurt out more senseless words to Keith, I gave all my mess to God.

Four hours. Five. I saw Heathcliff plodding and panting up the driveway.

"Heathcliff's home," I called to Keith in the loft.

Thank you, God. Thank you, thank you, thank you.

I ran down the driveway. "Oh, Heathcliff, good boy, Heathcliff, good boy, good boy." I hugged him. He hauled himself up the deck stairs and lay down. I leashed him and replenished the water in the outside bowl.

"Where's Freya," I asked, as if he'd be able to tell me. He panted, sighed a deep groan, and fell asleep.

I stood on the deck, keeping a lookout and praying. Thirty minutes later, Freya, muddy and panting, dragged herself up the driveway.

"Freya's home, too," I called to Keith.

Thank you, God. Thank you, thank you, thank you.

I waited at the top of the driveway. "Freya, where did you go? I was so worried." The words I'd said to Jessica when she returned home. Freya barely had enough energy for the hosing-off routine. "Good girl, Freya, good girl, good girl." After leashing her on the deck, I ran inside to make sure Keith had heard. Both of our dogs had come home.

They showed no interest in food that night but ate their kibble the following morning. When we dropped them at the kennel before heading to Farmville, Heathcliff jumped out and visited with the other dogs like they were buddies. Freya refused to leave the car. Keith had to walk her into the kennel and shut the gate behind him. She jumped at the fence gate, frantic to get back to him. The sight of her distress wrenched my heart. She was failing her trust test, too.

That evening, Keith's family gathered at the funeral parlor for Dad's viewing. As the two of us walked across the parking lot, the gentle rain soothed me. Dad's body looked as waxen as Keith's mom had in death, and my father, which didn't seem to bother anyone as they visited around. So, I followed suit, doing my best to support Keith and greet all—most of whom were strangers—and not get overwhelmed. ISFJ. For me, the highlight of the evening was the display of family pictures, a window into Keith's growing up years. Due to his family's frequent moves—Dad had been an Air Force fighter pilot—and Keith's marriages, Keith didn't have many personal items from his past, nothing like the treasure trove in my closet.

The next morning dawned warm and sunny with wisps of cirrus clouds. During the memorial service, I held Keith's hand and sat next to family members at the church-sponsored luncheon. Then Keith and I headed home to pick up the dogs. They barked with excitement and leaped into the back of the car. We fed them at home then went out for supper.

When we returned and the dogs did not meet us at the door, I knew something was wrong. Keith walked into the basement and called up the stairs. "Heathcliff, Freya, come, hurry-up." Then he sniffed. "We've got trouble."

Dog-mess puddled across the tile floor of the man cave. The volume told us both dogs were sick, no doubt from having eaten carrion. That explained their being gone five hours, plodding home, and refusing food. Now their dinners and both kinds of "hurry-ups" covered the basement floor.

While Keith tended to the dogs, I cleaned up the stinking mess and muttered, "This is Freya's fault."

The next morning, Freya seemed okay but not Heathcliff, so I took him to the vet for testing, rehydration, and antibiotics. Within two days, he recovered. When Freya messed in the basement again, I assumed she'd gone back for more and took her to the vet. She came home with antibiotics and medication for diarrhea.

During their recovery, Keith and I restricted the dogs' running. They got into trouble when they ran together, we observed, egging each other on. So, we reset the rules: they could run our mountain property off-leash, one at a time.

In early June, we took Heathcliff and Freya to see Mother in assisted care and celebrated her ninetieth birthday. Before the three-hour drive home, I gave the dogs a hurry-up. Freya never took her eyes off Keith and would not relieve herself. Separation from Keith negated trust in me. Half-way home, she piddled in the back of the car. We pulled into a gas station, and Keith led her on leash to finish emptying her bladder. Not one to miss an opportunity, Heathcliff jumped out, too, with me holding his leash. Keith with his girl, me with our boy.

For the rest of the drive home, Heathcliff sat in the back of the car and guarded. Freya rested her chin on the center console armrest and gave Keith her Princess Di look. I stroked her muzzle.

"Good girl, Freya, it's okay, good girl." But I knew she was a long way from trusting me, and I from trusting her. That pesky question again.

Trust, my stumbling block, the stepstone where I refused to place my feet.

Chapter 26

Fathers and Daughters

On Father's Day, neither of us had a father to call. No more Father Abraham. No more Dad. Alex called to wish Keith a happy Father's Day and confirm arrangements to meet in July for his grandfather's burial at Arlington National Cemetery. I'd already made hotel and kennel reservations.

I spent the day thinking about Father's Day memories, sorting through boxes and files, starting with the present Gretchen had given to her dad when she was in first grade. She'd taped her school picture onto the back of a piece of ruled manila paper and framed it by cutting a rectangle in the middle of her crayon drawing of a red apple with a green stem. On the lines above, along-side and below the drawing she printed:

On Father's Day
I like to say Thanks to dad In a special way!
From the "apple of your eye." Gretchen.

While tracing my fingers over her crayon and pencil strokes, I studied her photograph. She wore a blue and white smocked dress with white cuffed and puffed short-sleeves and a Peter Pan collar edged in lace. Her shiny blonde hair was pulled into a ponytail bun. Straight bangs covered her forehead and stray curls tickled the edges of her round cheeks and upturned smile. I saw her father's blue eyes, looking straight ahead, and her square jaw—his.

That was Father's Day in the alpha of her life. I picked up her last journal to read about the omega. The last words Gretchen and Keith spoke to one another, also on Father's Day.

*　*　*

June 18, 2001: "It is warm today, pleasant, hazy. Yesterday I called my father, and we spoke a little. He was oddly in tune with my train of thought. I'd mentioned casual relationships and how, no matter what you can do, sometimes responsibility ends. You can make a reasonable judgment about the results of certain behaviors, but eventually the sphere of your influence does finally end somewhere. For example, some random things people do, like 'acts of god.' I remembered aloud that long-ago party where a young man smashed himself to pieces not long after his drunken leave-taking... the keys glittering past me for a heart stopping instant as they sailed over the balcony railing. I did nothing. I held my tongue. I did not reach out. I do not, did not know him. In that spare moment where my sphere of influence might possibly have intersected with his own, I failed this man. My father seemed surprised to hear me worry over these things, even if a stranger's crippling could not reasonably be considered my responsibility. He seemed proud of me, and it filled me with shame.

"The other things we spoke of, how we exist, and we don't know why... why these particles join and separate as they do and why their interactions evolve consciousness. There are metaphysical implications to this but mostly we spoke of the unknown physical mechanism. We are only the sum of our parts, our experiences, all this organic learning, but if that sum seems greater than it should be it's only because we don't understand our own parts.

"I enjoyed this conversation, much like the ones we've had since I was smaller. He told me work stories, visiting stories, house stories. I love stories. They are some of the best and most interesting things about people.

"This was an excellent goodbye."

* * *

I remembered reading about that long-ago party the first time at Black-water Falls. She'd gotten drunk on beer and wine. What happened next haunted me, but not in the same way, not anymore. No anger, no jealousy, no judgment. Only sadness to think shame was among Gretchen's last memories. Guilt that was not guilt at all because she'd done nothing wrong, yet felt she'd behaved dishonorably. In her view, she had failed to do her duty.

"I did nothing," she wrote. "I held my tongue. I did not reach out. I failed this man."

She had not stopped a young man from leaving a party drunk and crashing his motorcycle. Memory of the young motorcyclist on the Baltimore Beltway stirred, how his sphere of influence had almost crashed into mine. But that wasn't the connection. Then I thought about the man who hurt Mother and how my sphere of influence might have intersected with theirs but hadn't.

And there it was. Oh, Gretchen, I said inside my heart, I understand this shame—doing nothing and failing someone. Maybe someday I'll tell your father my real secret. But I want you to know you were loved, are loved. You were and are a blessing. The apple of your father's eye.

The apple of his eye. Sitting at my desk, I thought about the last time I talked with Daddy, also on Father's Day, five years before Gretchen said goodbye to her father. I was living in Texas and had called to wish my father a happy Father's Day. We chatted about what he was reading and planned to write. He hadn't been able to do much of anything since the right-brain stroke felled him a decade before, years of degradation and suffering. As a child, growing up on his parents' farm, he'd done the work of an adult. Work was who he was. Now that and so much more had been stripped away.

"When are you, Jessica, and David coming to visit?" he asked.

"Next month." I told him about my students' summer internships and how excited his grandchildren were about the summer workshop performance at the Tuzer Dance Center—Jessica and David both danced, ballet, tap, and jazz. Words, words, words. I jabbered about my successes, those "never enough" attempts to earn his love and attention.

When I finished talking, he said, "Carole, I am honored to be your father."

"Thank you, Daddy, I am honored to be your daughter."

He died five days later in a hospital bed Mother had moved into their bedroom. The next step would have been a nursing home, which Daddy didn't want. But there was nothing anyone could do to help him, no more options. So, after ten years of tending to him and his illnesses, Mother let him go.

Now, on Father's Day seventeen years later, I felt remorse. As I held Gretchen's last journal in my hand, I told myself the truth. The last conversation I'd had with my father was not an excellent goodbye. I had interpreted our last words as making amends, but mine were tainted with grudge. I had not forgiven my Father Abraham for what I perceived as his betrayals and abandonment.

I walked upstairs to the small closet in the loft where I now kept my memories and retrieved the photo album Mother had made for me. Graduation weekend, Wheaton College, Massachusetts, May 1973. Inducted into Phi Beta Kappa, played flute in the Senior Recital, graduated Magna cum Laude, the same honors as Jane. She, her husband, my parents, Leslie, and Mother's sister attended the ceremonies and events in which I was the center of attention. I allowed myself to think I'd finally appeased the god of numbers that measured my worth. I allowed myself to think, for a moment, I had become the apple of my father's eye.

Daddy escorted me to the Father-Daughter reception on the back lawn of the President's House. I wore a long, flowered dress and navy-blue blazer with a white carnation pinned to the lapel. In the photograph, I squint toward the sun. The shadow of Jane's camera-holding husband darkens the grass to my right. Four feet to my left, Daddy stands in his tan slacks, maroon shirt, wide striped tie, and cream-colored jacket. His teeth and fists clench. Was he nervous in this formal setting, as I was? Or was I reading my own thoughts into his expression?

Other pictures in the album featured me in cap and gown, with my roommate, our friends, and various family groupings. My mother and sisters wore tight smiles like my father's, or frowns, heads bowed, eyes downcast. Were they bored by the long weekend—graduations are notoriously boring—or were other things happening?

Our graduations ended my parents' child raising years of hard-fought, loving sacrifice. Mother adjusted, returning to school and teaching. Daddy, however, seemed to have a difficult time as his girls grew up and left home. Before each of our weddings, he built and rebuilt sections of stone wall along the road in front of our house as monuments to my sisters and me, leading to crippling bursitis in his elbows. Was he shoring up walls and enduring physical pain so he wouldn't feel the heartache of our leaving? Maybe he saw his daughters' adulthood as a harbinger of his own decline. Or maybe he didn't want to let his children go.

Throughout graduation weekend, I gave no thought to anyone's ambivalence except my own. I had no prospects, no teaching job and no ring on my finger, not even a boyfriend. Though I'd backed away from the edge where the poisonous demon lurked, in truth, worshipping the god of numbers had consumed me. When I walked across the stage erected in the grassy Dimple of Old Campus and received my diploma, the honors and achievements felt meaningless. I felt atrophied, less confident, and less myself than when I'd left home four years ago. And yet, stepping off stage, I looked toward my parents, hoping to see them applauding, hoping to have earned my father's love.

My father's chair was empty.

Was he running around taking the other pictures in my album, or did my brother-in-law take them? After the ceremony ended, we couldn't find Daddy—he had disappeared. People were leaving, and I remembered my family wondering how they were going to get home, since he had the car keys. At the time, I assumed he was not able to celebrate my success, because that weekend my star outshone his. Bootstrapping from poor, backwoods farm boy in a one-room schoolhouse to world-renowned Professor of Pediatrics and Medical Sociology at Yale University had earned him success but no honors on his diplomas. Now yet another daughter had outachieved him in school. As the parking lot cleared, he reappeared. Not a word was spoken.

He hadn't expected me to do this well in school or even finish, or so I assumed given what happened the summer before I left home. One afternoon, Daddy called me into his study. On his desk piled with academic manuscripts and financial documents, he produced a bill.

"Tuition insurance, should I pay it? If you get married or drop out, I'll lose a lot of money." This was not the voice of my beloved Father Abraham, was it? Maybe Mother was right: maybe he did think women weren't as smart as men.

I glanced at the sizable number on the bill, looked at my father, and curled my lip. "Tuition insurance is a waste of money. I have no plans to get married. I think you have to be dating someone seriously, right?" The sarcasm in my voice came from a person I didn't want to know. My father and I said no more.

I closed the photo album. Too bad I hadn't wanted to know him better—or myself through his eyes. And now it was too late to ask. Too late, too bad.

Had I been unfair to him all these years? Maybe Daddy was overcome with emotion at my graduation and afraid of weeping in public. Or maybe he was just looking for a men's room.

Why hadn't I asked? Was I afraid of the answer? Perhaps I latched onto the first explanation, because anger was easier than facing the alternative. Disappointment in myself for setting academic success as my only goal, the Narrowest Margin of Victory, as Gretchen called it. Disappointment that I wasn't the apple of my father's eye—and should not have been.

I returned the photo album to the closet, shut the door, and sighed. Daddy was a good father, remarkable in so many ways. He did enough, he was enough, more than enough. I thought about the first blog post I'd published, remembering Daddy on Father's Day. How the child in me adored him, then and now. But my body's tightness told a different story. I had chosen not to give up my grudge; I was choosing not to forgive the past. The Spirit showed me the missing piece in my faith—forgiveness—but knew I wasn't ready to give or receive it.

Why did I want him to be perfect? Like father, like daughter. How long until I would be able to leave it?

Soon, I hoped, so I could honestly and truly say, *Thanks to Dad in a special way.*

Chapter 27

Seeking the Truth

Looking back, I see the regrets about my father likely prompted me to seek information about the attack on my mother. I didn't want another "too late, too bad" relationship if I could help it. Selfishly, I also wanted to know the truth before my mother died, the same as when I got baptized before my father died. And after a lifetime of lost opportunities, I was tired of not knowing what happened that day.

So, one morning in early July, I emailed the librarian at the *New Haven Register*: "I wonder if there is an archived article or articles related to the incident involving my mother Joyce Duff in March 1957. If so, could I obtain a copy/copies? I have also contacted the Woodbridge Police in hopes of obtaining the police report. Thank you so much."

I signed the email and clicked send without expecting an immediate reply. As a historian, I knew research meant waiting. I'd give it a month then follow up.

A second round of seeking began soon after, this time with Keith. We were eating breakfast on the dining deck, our first summer full-time at Vanaprastha. The rising sun painted the Rockfish Valley with Impressionist colors: crimson, cobalt blue, viridian, emerald green, and chrome yellow. After a year of navigating one stepstone at a time, I felt settled now—more like plateaued. Wasn't I supposed to be reinventing myself and building a new life here?

Keith apparently shared my thoughts because out of the blue he said, "We need to have some fun, Carole, invite new friends for drinks and hors d'oeuvres or a meal. Let's find some nice restaurants. I hear there're great places to eat in Charlottesville and Staunton."

I studied Keith's full head of white hair. Grey streaked my hair now—I no longer covered that sign of aging with highlights or dye. I thought about Gretchen and our parents and what Keith often said. We only get so much time on this earth, and we rarely know how long or short our lives will be. Time is the most valuable thing we have.

"Shall I order annual passes to the American Shakespeare Center today?" I asked. We'd been looking at advertisements for a while. "We could combine a show at the theater with lunch or dinner in Staunton." I passed my empty plate to Keith.

"Sounds good to me. We should have a date-night every month." He scraped leftover bits of scrambled eggs from the pan, dividing them between his plate and mine. Heathcliff and Freya—both leash-tethered—perked up.

As Keith stood, a plate in each hand, the dogs moved to their feeding area on the main deck and sat, eyes on Keith, tails wagging left and right like synchronized windshield wipers. Keith set the plates down on either side of the water bowl. The dogs struggled to keep their noses from following the food. Drool dripped from their mouths. Freya licked her chops.

"Okay." Keith waved his hand down, and the dogs nosedived for the plates. I sighed. If only I could enjoy life as dogs do: grateful, in the moment, humble to our master, obedient, patient, and able to wait.

Keith returned to the dining deck and his train of thought. "Let's find a new church, one grounded in scripture with an emphasis on growth. I'm not growing."

I knew a change would be good for me, too, given my church background—or lack thereof. I'd been comfortable, sitting in the pews of a nearby church, hearing 'God is Love' messages. Comfortable instead of wrestling with Bible verses, which might challenge me. I thought about what Keith had said about creativity, how growth comes from new experiences, being a novice, and acknowledging ignorance. Digging deeper into the onion layers, climbing steep mountains, lifting weights that make us sweat.

"Next Sunday, let's try the service and Bible study at the Lutheran church in Waynesboro." Over the Blue Ridge Mountains into the Shenandoah Valley. "I know you wanted to stay local, and yes, it's a drive. But let's see how we like it."

Pastor Tim Bohlmann of Bethany Lutheran Church was about fifteen years our junior, sharp-eyed, energetic, and engaging. We found the community friendly. During services, I sat comfortably in the red-velvet cushioned pews—as long as I let the message fly over my head.

One Sunday in mid-July, Pastor Tim was out of town, and his father Gordon, a retired Lutheran missionary, served as guest pastor. Pastor Gordon spoke about perfection—or rather the impossibility of human perfection on this earth—and about sin, judgment, and redemption. Did I attend to his words because of what I'd told Keith about my breakdown and perfectionism? Maybe, and perhaps there was some awareness on my part about the distinction between human-motivated perfectionism and God's perfection, I'm not sure. I remember thinking about some of C.S. Lewis's assertions: Rousseau was wrong, we are not good. We have free will, but there is no hope of getting where you want to go except by going God's way. Then I recalled Flannery O'Connor's blunt statement about faith: "Either one is serious about salvation, or one is not."

While listening to Pastor Gordon's message, I scribbled notes on the back of the church bulletin. Suddenly, I realized I had not made the paradigm shift. I wanted it both ways. I believed in God and accepted the Spirit's guidance but only as long as I stayed in my comfort zone, calm and in control.

The next day, I wrote a blog post, quoting O'Connor and others' words but offering few of my own. I clicked publish and closed my laptop. Contradiction explained. Inconsistency resolved. I pushed back from my desk and sighed with relief. The Spirit knew I'd side-stepped. Part of me knew, too—denial being a means to maintain control. Indeed, I had not made the paradigm shift, but I was getting frighteningly close.

My blog post topics had changed in the past two years. After determining the main topic areas, I subtitled *Notes from Vanaprastha* as "reflections about faith, nature, and writing" and categorized and subcategorized my posts accordingly. If I'd paid attention, I would have noticed faith posts far outnumbered all the other categories combined.

Sure enough, a month after I'd emailed the librarian at the *New Haven Register*, I received a reply. "Hi Carole," she wrote. "I am putting in the mail copies of the articles I have on file under the name of your mom's attacker, Carl Wilson. I hope these will be helpful and not cause any undue grief."

Carl Wilson. I stared at the name. Carl Wilson. Had I heard his name before? I tilted my head to the side. Maybe, maybe not, I wasn't sure. Maybe like Mother I hadn't wanted to remember, so I could live all those years in a crime scene and pretend life was comfortably predictable like Angela Lansbury in TV's *Murder She Wrote*. But now that I knew his name—finally—I wanted to learn as much as I could about the crime that changed my family's life.

When the much-anticipated packet from the *New Haven Register* arrived, I immediately sat down at my desk, ripped open the envelope, and sorted the articles, studying the photographs and reading the stories in chronological order. No ambivalence. The truth—finally.

March 28, 1957, the day after the attack, "Burglary Is Held Motive In Woodbridge Shooting," the headline read. The article featured a photograph of Carl Wilson in handcuffs and a policeman standing in front of the breezeway of our house. They stood where I'd stood when my mother hung out the breezeway door and said, "Don't rebel, don't rebel," before I left home for college. They stood where I stood in my recurrent dream, when the plane crashed in the field in front of our house. I shifted, uncomfortable in my chair, then stilled my body and studied the photograph again. Through the breezeway window on the left was the table where my sisters and I kept our treasures: shiny silver milk-bottle caps and quartz rocks sparkling with mica. The police had confiscated our rocks as potential weapons.

"They must not have children," Daddy had scoffed when explaining why our treasures were gone. Visible through the window to the right of the breezeway door was the top of an aluminum folding lawn-chair. On the wall above, Daddy had hung twine for Mother to display the pictures Jane and I drew, fastened with clothespins. I sighed. Our perfect world had been built on a Big Rock Candy Mountain, the comforting song Howie always sang while painting the houses and barns on Round Hill Farm. Not the Depression-Era version but Burl Ives, singing about the land of milk and honey: *where the lemonade springs and the bluebird sings in that Big Rock Candy Mountain*. Then one day everything changed for us girls. Like Adam and Eve, after eating the apple from the Tree of Knowledge, we learned the world was not all sweet. We learned about evil, guilt, and death.

Setting the articles aside, I emailed my sisters and asked if they would be willing to tell me what they remembered. They must have been curious, too, because both responded with memories and requests for copies of the articles. As the oldest, Jane remembered the most. Leslie contributed other online articles. We shared a few stories we'd believed, now discounted by the facts. Without the truth, a child's mind takes all kinds of strange side trips.

In my memory closet, I discovered a brief description among my father's papers, which he wrote during his stroke years, and I kept after he died. With his account, my sisters' memories, and mine—and the newspaper articles spread across my desk—I started writing the story I'd been trying to tell from the beginning of my reinvention, the story that had bled through the Gretchen excerpt I took to my first writing class. Now I realized she had been the catalyst the Spirit used to guide me toward the truth.

The truth. Finally.

While writing this account, I felt the distance between my five-year-old self and the adult I'd become shrink. My wait was almost over. Two rounds of seeking, past and present, were converging.

Chapter 28

Wednesday, March 27, 1957

I stared at my laptop screen, fighting the urge to change the subject and flee. Writing our family's story would break the silence we'd carefully maintained—I'd carefully maintained over the years. Instead of mute avoidance of the past, I wanted to remember but dreaded the remembering. *Keep going,* the Spirit told me, *there's something better on the other side of that mountain.* So, I kept climbing, falling, and getting up, putting one foot in front of the other.

Climbing and remembering that without God's help, I would not have become a teacher.

Or survived a failed marriage.

Or married Keith.

Or dared to face my family's ordeal.

Or written this.

At noon on Wednesday, March 27, 1957, Carl Wilson, 23, of Bristol, Connecticut left his job at a die-casting factory in Plantsville and drove south on Route 8 in a late model aquamarine Buick. Though hunting season was closed, he had his hunting license pinned to his jacket and a 12-gauge double-barreled pump action shotgun under the front seat. It was a warm, sunny day. Maple trees budded red. Birds sang mating calls.

Aimless, Carl drove toward New Haven, an area where he had never lived or worked. Exiting Route 8 at Seymour, he passed the Dairy Queen and turned in the direction of Woodbridge. Minutes later, he veered onto Sanford Road. He stopped at the intersection with Newton and spotted a ranch-style house perched atop a gentle hill.

WEDNESDAY, MARCH 27, 1957

Carl drove by three times and, seeing no car in the yard, decided no one was home.

He parked on Newton near Meadowbrook Road. Taking a roll of white cloth adhesive tape from a first aid kit in his trunk, he tore off three patches, and stuck them on his face to disguise himself. Then he closed the trunk and pulled out his 12-gauge. With shotgun in hand, Carl Wilson strolled up our driveway.

At 3:45 p.m., he rang the breezeway doorbell.

"What do you want?" Mother asked the slim, baby-faced man, standing outside the breezeway door. Hunters were uncommon but not unusual in this rural part of town.

"I thought my friend lived here," Carl said. "Could you check his name and address in the telephone directory?"

Because there was no lock on the breezeway door, Mother locked the door between the kitchen and breezeway. She went to look up the information but found no such name. While she was gone, Carl Wilson stepped into the breezeway.

Mother returned and unlocked the kitchen door. Then she heard our younger sister Leslie calling from her crib, "Mommy, Mommy. I want to get up now."

Carl moved toward Mother. "Be quiet," he said.

She stiffened, blocking his path into the house and to my younger sister.

Carl panicked. He pointed his 12-gauge at Mother's face. His finger slid onto the trigger.

She pushed the muzzle down. The first shot tore into Mother's right knee, nearly severing her leg. She fell back, screaming and struggling to take the shotgun away from him.

He jerked the shotgun up, out of her grasp. The second shot punched a hole in the corner of the breezeway ceiling.

Flipping the muzzle around, Carl clubbed her head so hard the buttstock split in two. At five-foot-two and 110 pounds, bleeding and beaten, Mother braced herself against the frame of the kitchen door.

Carl rushed out of the breezeway, down our driveway, and up the road to his car. At that moment, ten-year-old Ricky Burroughs and Peter Halsey stepped off the school bus at Meadowbrook Road.

"What 'cha doing, Mister?" Ricky asked, seeing Carl's shotgun.

"Hunting, just killed a squirrel," Carl said. "Left it up the road—you can have it."

Suspicious, Ricky wrote down the Buick's license number. Carl Wilson drove home to Bristol to eat dinner with his pretty young wife and thirteen-month-old son.

Mother dragged herself up the breezeway steps to the kitchen then crawled across the dining room and living room into the master bedroom, leaving a blood trail the full length of the house. She reached for the telephone and misdialed the number for the police. Then she called Mrs. Taffel whose family lived in a rental house on Sanford Road, the next school bus stop.

"Help, please help me, Helen. I've been shot. Please don't leave me here to die."

Because Jane's second-grade Brownie Troop met that day, I got off the bus with the Taffel children instead of the boys at Meadowbrook and walked home by myself. A lone dog barked far down Newton Road. I glanced at our white clapboard green-shuttered house on the hill and pondered which section of the stone wall I'd climb to shortcut across the field past our vegetable garden.

Mrs. Taffel rushed outside, gathered her children, and called to me, "Come back, Carole."

I retraced my steps, smiling, because I thought Mrs. Taffel was inviting me to play with her children. After calling the police, she instructed her oldest to keep us inside. Jetty and Silver guarded while Mrs. Taffel ran to help Mother.

When the police arrived, Mrs. Taffel carried Leslie back to her house on Sanford Road. Two officers accompanied Mother in the ambulance, speeding to St. Raphael Hospital in New Haven. "Get my husband, get my husband," she yelled. Upon arrival at St. Raphael's, a priest gave her Last Rites.

Two policemen arrived at my father's office at Grace-New Haven Hospital. They stood right up close, questioning him about his whereabouts in the past several hours, ready to arrest him. After determining he was not the perpetrator, they took him to see Mother. She had never lost consciousness and was worried about us girls. Daddy assured her we were fine.

Connecticut State Police led the manhunt, erecting roadblocks on all area roads. Our neighbors gathered at the Halseys' house across the road from our home. Mrs. Taffel called Jane's Brownie leader to make sure she and Mrs. Taffel's same-age daughter got dropped off at the Halseys'.

The adults whispered in the kitchen, glanced out the windows, and told us children to be quiet. We huddled in a dark, pine-paneled room

WEDNESDAY, MARCH 27, 1957

with a shade-drawn window, watching TV and eating peanut butter and marshmallow fluff sandwiches for supper. Jane walked around, asking where Leslie was and what was going on. Finally, Mrs. Taffel brought Leslie out from a back bedroom and told us Mother had been hurt.

We saw police cars in our driveway and along the road and overheard the adults say, "They got him. Ricky Burroughs helped catch him." He had given the police the license plate number.

At 6:25 p.m., four state and local police officers arrested Carl Wilson at his apartment in Bristol. They had located his car parked nearby and found the broken shotgun under the front seat. Carl surrendered without resistance. He admitted to attempted burglary of our home and, after an all-night interrogation, confessed to Mother's brutal shooting and beating.

That night while Mother was in surgery, Leslie cried in a playpen next to Jane and me on a sofa bed in the Taffels' living room. Daddy arrived in his hospital whites. He had talked the police guards at our house into letting him get Leslie's favorite stuffed animal, a dog. Without turning on the light, Daddy bent over the playpen, soothing and quieting Leslie. Then he left to stay with Mother through the night.

During a four-hour emergency operation, the doctors at St. Raphael Hospital saved my mother's life and, in a first-of-its-kind procedure, reattached her leg. Mother received many units of blood from the blood bank, a debt my father spent years repaying by donating his own.

The next morning, Mother was listed in fair condition. She was moved to a regular room at Grace-New Haven Hospital. "Life must go on," she told my father.

Daddy brought clothes for Jane and me to wear to school—the police had let him into the house again. But we couldn't go home until they finished their investigation and gave Howie permission to remove the blood-soaked rugs and clean Mother's blood off the floors.

"Mommy's really dead, isn't she, Daddy." Jane's voice was gut low.

My father grimaced.

Jane and I washed our faces, brushed our teeth, and combed our hair. We donned school dresses, clean underwear, socks, and shoes. Then we waited for the bus with the Taffel children.

I saved the draft and reread my father's brief account. He wrote about my mother, lying on the master bedroom floor, waiting for help to arrive. "She told me she could think of only one thing in light of me and our dependent children: 'What a crummy way to die.'"

A lump formed in my throat. I couldn't swallow. In my head, I saw my mother's body, broken and bleeding, and heard her say, "What a crummy way to die." Then I wept for Mother, my Father Abraham, and my sisters. What a crummy thing to happen—and for what?

I wiped my face, blew my nose, and went through the newspaper articles again. "Savage Crime Rocks Friends," the headline from the April 7, 1957 issue of the *New Britain Sunday Herald* stated. "He Tried to Do Right."

I tried to do right, too, but I didn't.

If you tell the truth, you're dead—Gretchen's words echoed in my head. So be it, I told her, because if I don't tell the truth, I'm worse than dead. No. More. Secrets.

Chapter 29

The Real Secret

I hunched over my desk, a sixty-two-year-old woman, battling self-pity and self-loathing. In the past, whenever I'd tried to write about the days after my mother's attack, that's what spewed onto the page. So, I prayed for the Spirit to guide me back to the fearful unhinged mind of my five-year-old kindergarten self. Her story, without pity or loathing, then my secret—the dangerous truth I'd never spoken and desperately needed to tell.

The morning after the assault, Jane and I got off the bus at Center School, in the common area across from the Congregational church and next to the Woodbridge Town Hall, which in those years also housed the police station. I figured news of the attack had traveled around the town square, and everyone knew. All day at school, I kept my head bowed and studied my shoes. I imagined teachers and school mates pointing at me and whispering, "She's the one whose mother was shot."

When Jane and I got home, Mother's oldest brother and Grammy were there—they'd driven through the night from northern Maine. Grammy was a widow, tall, erect, and rail thin, her grey hair netted and pinned, a silent woman shaped by poverty and cold New England winters. Grammy told us to be quiet, our uncle was sleeping. Jane and I changed from our school dresses to play clothes. We noticed all the rugs were missing and the master bedroom furniture had been moved into the living room so Howie could strip and refinish the floor.

"Howie shellacked the floor in your parents' bedroom," Grammy said. "The floor's wet. Don't go in there." She shut the door to the empty room and returned to the kitchen.

I stared at the closed door. My parents kept allowance coins in a ceramic candy dish on the fireplace mantel on the far side of their bedroom. Without my weekly allowance, I couldn't buy chewing gum or cinnamon fireballs at the gas station or grocery store checkout.

Ever so slowly, I opened the door until I could see the candy dish on the mantel across the room. The promise of coins and sweet-tasting candy overrode the lacquered smell of wet shellac. I stepped into the room. For a moment, my body floated numb and weightless as I'd hoped. Then reality pulled me back to earth, and I sprawled across the sticky wet floor.

Grammy must have heard me fall because she came running. She grabbed my arm and pulled me off the floor into the living room. Then she burst into fury.

"Didn't. I. Tell. You. NOT to go in there? Didn't. You. Hear. Me?" As Grammy scrubbed shellac off my hands, face, and hair, each swipe of the wet washcloth marked time with her words like the crisp beat of a conductor's baton. "Now, look what a mess you've made." She pointed to my flannel shirt, corduroy pants, and the master bedroom floor.

I cried for all the trouble I'd caused. I cried for the sweets I wouldn't be able to buy. I cried for wanting my mother—not this bony, chin-bristled stranger. I cried for my mother, who was "really dead" in the hospital.

Because policies restricted hospital visitation, especially for children, Daddy asked his superior in the Department of Pediatrics to declare an emergency visit. They granted his request and one Sunday morning, Daddy spirited the three of us up the back stairs. I wore the pale-yellow crinoline dress Jane had outgrown. She carried a pot of tulips; I carried a hyacinth plant; Daddy carried Leslie. The sound of two little girls' black patent leather shoes echoed down the long, dark, antiseptic corridors.

As the door opened to her room, I saw white: Mother in bed wrapped in white blankets, her head in white bandages, her leg in a full white cast suspended by white pulley ropes. Leslie had mud on her sneakers, but nobody stopped her from climbing into bed and snuggling with Mother. Jane and Daddy stood beside the hospital bed. Mother spoke faintly, saying she was glad to see us.

My body travelled to some distant place. Cold and numb. I thought about all I had seen and heard, what I had done and had not done the day a man came to rob our house, and he hurt my mother.

You should have saved your mother, an inner voice scolded. *You should have gone home instead of thinking about playing with the Taffels.*

THE REAL SECRET

I bowed my head and accepted this secret verdict.
Guilty.

My real secret. Shame like Gretchen's. She did not reach for a drunken boy's keys; I did not go home to save my mother. We both failed someone when they needed help. And we'd been happy. Happy while playing and having fun. Happy while someone lay injured and dying. Happy while not doing what we could and should have done.

I wept for Gretchen and my younger self. For the happy five-year-old girls we'd been until our perfect worlds fell apart. For the young adults we'd become. Blaming ourselves for a broken world and desperately trying to regain perfection. Having wept for my family and myself, I now wept for the others hurt that day: Mrs. Taffel, Grammy, and Howie. I imagined Mrs. Taffel receiving the phone call and seeing her friend's body, bloody and broken. I imagined Grammy also receiving a phone call, and her oldest son driving all night from northern Maine. Grammy had swallowed her fear for her child so she could take care of three confused and frightened little girls. I imagined Howie, cleaning up Mother's blood. So much blood. Blood everywhere. Never had I allowed myself to see these images, smell the fears, hear the thoughts, touch the feelings, taste the reality of being in those terrible moments. To hold them and my confusion together in my head, heart, and body.

It took me days to reestablish the professional distance I needed to revise the entire draft. Then one morning in late August, I emailed the file to Keith—we regularly exchanged writing and edited each other's pieces. He already knew the basic story and what Mother had told me two or three years before. About how others thought this could never happen to them, and how her doctor said she was their first limb reattachment. But by the time Keith finished reading the draft, he would know. My real secret. What would he think of the writing, the story? Of me?

At dinner, after he prayed, I asked, "Did you get a chance to read the piece I sent you?" I felt a small twinge in my chest. Rather than feedback, I wanted discernment. He discerned that, too.

"Yes—I just sent you my review." His voice softened. "Every child comes to the realization about death, becoming aware of how fragile their world is. Yours did not come gently. Neither did mine."

He spoke about his family, based in Okinawa in the mid-50s when he was nine years old. While playing 'Army' one day on the cliffs near their home, he'd found the tripod mount for a machine gun fixed in a cave entrance and a human jawbone inside the cave. World War II relics.

"All I thought was this jawbone used to be a human being. This jawbone is what I am. I didn't speak for days. My mother thought perhaps I was sick. I didn't tell her what happened until years later." I imagined Keith as a fourth grader, as in the family pictures at Dad's viewing.

I nodded. "I kept my feelings secret, too, and suspect most children do. It's a lot to take in, that our parents will die and so will we."

We ate in silence, perhaps each of us lost in our own memories. Then I took a chance. "Even now, I feel guilty for not going home that day, for not saving her." The real secret buried for decades.

Keith looked straight at me. "Carole, if you went home that day, your mother would have had another child to protect, and that might have ended her life."

I cocked my head. "Huh, I never thought about that before. And if Jane didn't have Scouts, we would have gotten off the bus at Meadowbrook. We would have seen Carl Wilson. We both would have gone home. Then Mother would have had all three of her children to protect. Oh, my goodness. What blessings! God really was watching out for us that day."

Overwhelming joy flowed over me. Then suddenly, the dream about the plane crash in front of our house made sense—the stone wall I didn't climb, the field I didn't cross, our garden with bleeding tomatoes, calls for help and never being able to rescue anyone. It all made sense.

Without knowing it, the five-year-old child in me had been reenacting the past from a safe distance, trying to rewrite the event, hoping for a different end.

The next morning, as I reviewed Keith's edits and suggestions on my draft, I thought about the field in front of our house again and remembered. The grasshopper. This time, my overwhelming feeling was not joy but horror. After years of avoiding the past, the adult in me had worked her way back to it. That day, in blinding rage, I had lashed out against an innocent. My beastly rage had surfaced other times, too—the reason why that silly story still haunted me. At that moment, the memory of the Baltimore Beltway motorcyclist returned in vivid detail. This time, I saw the connection—the time lapse and now the lesson. Am I any different from this man, racing ahead regardless of consequences? No. Because to get what I want—control—I'm willing to risk hurting others.

THE REAL SECRET

Dear God, another guilty secret.

I felt trapped in a whack-a-mole game. As I whacked one guilty secret down, another popped up. And I had no idea how to stop playing the game.

Chapter 30

Both Sinner and Saint

Eventually, I would find the answer to ending whack-a-mole guilt in the parable of the prodigal son. In truth, I'm still plumbing the depths of the parable. And, as with the gift of teaching after my breakdown in college and the blessing of Keith after my failed marriage, the answer would come after a devastating fall, as in Richard Rohr's *Falling Upward*.

My fall upward began after Labor Day when Keith and I enrolled in the Basics and Beginnings class for membership at Bethany Lutheran Church. We met with others new to the church in the basement Fellowship Room on Sunday after the 11 o'clock service. Pastor's topics were basic for people like Keith, raised in the faith.

But not for me. I'd never attended a class like this, not even before baptism.

Simul justus et peccator, Pastor's handout stated, quoting Martin Luther. Both sinner and saint. The hard metal of the folding chair pressed cold against my spine. I gritted my teeth in a rictus smile and folded my hands in several different positions. Wasn't I serious about faith? Wasn't this what I wanted? What was stopping me? Hadn't I crossed the Rubicon by deciding to believe in God and listening to the Spirit's guidance? Hadn't I explored the topic of perfection in my blog post and resolved the issue?

You that are simple, turn in here! Was that Wisdom or Folly? In Proverbs 9, Wisdom and Folly summoned people with the same words. Why? *Lay aside immaturity, and live, and walk in the way of insight*, Lady Wisdom said. Insight, wasn't that what I wanted? *To come to be what you are not, you must go by a way in which you are not*, wrote John of the Cross. Wasn't that what I'd been doing, going where the Spirit led me? Why this confusion? I felt like two selves wrestled inside me. The split made little sense. But it would.

The next day, I emailed Pastor Tim and requested an appointment.

We met in Pastor's inner office, a spacious, high-ceilinged room with light shining through a wall of windows behind his desk. I perched on the edge of a sofa near the door, crossed my legs at the ankles, folded my hands, and squared my shoulders. Pastor Tim pulled a chair from around the small meeting table and placed it near the sofa, close enough to attend without boxing me in. I studied the Basics and Beginnings worksheet I'd marked with questions written in the margin like a lesson plan. Running my pen down the page, I noted each of the numbered points. I stilled myself and started with point number one.

"Keith wants to join this church, but I'm not ready." I shifted uncomfortably. "I wasn't raised this way." Back to my childhood? Where did that come from? Already off-script. I rattled on about my atheist upbringing, how my father told me God is dead, and we called him Father Abraham in a loving, teasing way. Pastor listened without comment.

"Then twenty years ago, when I was in my early forties and my marriage failed, I fell apart." Was I really telling a complete stranger about my humiliation? My chest tightened, and horror crept into my throat, but I couldn't stop talking.

"It happened once before, in college." The breakdown, too?

I swallowed hard and looked at my script. "Thank goodness, I found a mission—teaching. But it wasn't until my divorce that I decided to believe in God. Eventually, I felt guided and peaceful." Back on track. "My children and I attended a large church. The pastor spoke about God's love. I felt comfortable, and my children and I got baptized." My body eased.

Pastor looked straight at me. "You checked that box."

I nodded my head because what he said was true. We got baptized to join the church. I figured he'd heard stories like mine many times—people going through the motions without understanding the meaning—and I also knew he had suffered a fall. Years ago, his two-year-old son had a series of strokes, which stole his voice and more. Pastor's son would never be able to leave home. When I looked into Pastor Tim's eyes, I saw someone I could trust.

"I thought of baptism as a way of choosing God in a public way, though it still felt as if I was betraying my Father Abraham." Abandoning him, my childhood idol. My muscles tensed.

"People come to church for many reasons. It's not for me to judge." Pastor's words both reassured and encouraged. I sensed the paradigm shift, reached into the heart of danger, and for a brief moment grasped the truth about my split self, resulting in immediate insight.

I called myself a Christian but was not. I was a prodigal and a fake.

"But I got the sacrament all wrong." My voice shook. I couldn't sit still. Maybe I'd gotten everything wrong. I dropped the pen and paper in my lap. My hands leaped into the air as if by their own volition. "I don't know anything about the New Testament. I don't know anything about Jesus Christ. I don't understand sin. I don't understand suffering."

I took a deep breath and wailed like a child. "I want my comfort back!" The comfort of God's love and the Spirit's guidance, not this terrible unmasked me.

Pastor Tim likely didn't know what he was dealing with but didn't let me off the hook. Thank God. "I understand that. Faith gives us God's perfect grace. But there's tension in life between imperfection and perfection. Our humanity means imperfection."

"Well yes, of course." My dual manner shifted from my gut back to my head. "Nobody's perfect," I said, though I still wanted to be.

"We're works in progress," Pastor said. "But if we try to hide our imperfections, we run into sin right away." Hiding mistakes. How did he know that about me?

"Be patient," he said. "Life is a Both-And paradox. We are both sinful in nature yet saint in redemption—that's the tension."

I glanced at the words printed on the Basics and Beginnings worksheet in my lap again. *Simul justus et peccator.* Both righteous and sinful. Sinner and saint. This time my hackles went up. Well, I'm no saint. But a sinner? Not me. I'm good and right and strong.

But I didn't feel that way.

Suddenly, my head and heart merged. I came face to face with my inner judge—the Grand Inquisitor of sins I hadn't committed and defender of sins I had—and saw a liar. Folly. I had mistaken Folly's lies for Wisdom's truth, just as Proverbs 9 warned. I had deceived myself.

My heart raced, my brain ratcheted, and my gut constricted, tighter, tighter, still tighter. Decades-old defenses, which had bolstered my identity, crumbled. "I'm feeling exposed," I said. Cracked open. Dying. My hands and knees trembled uncontrollably. Then my entire body shook, both hot and cold. The poisonous demon, on full display, right there in the Pastor's office.

I saw Pastor Tim watching me. My throat clenched. "I'm having an anxiety attack," I said. I was barely able to breathe and desperately afraid of shrieking.

"Yes, I can see that, and I'm praying for you." Was he ever going to let me off the hook? No, that's not why I came. He knows what I want: the missing piece of my faith.

Pastor shifted in his chair. "Great love means great suffering. The tension between love and suffering exists within us. We try to do good, but our human side always falls short."

Falling short—he knew that about me, too. "I've lived with that almost all my life," I said with no small amount of self-pity. Both relieved and fearful I'd shake out of my shoes or worse, dissolve into tears, I told him about Mother's attack. I didn't mention God's blessings that day—the blessings never crossed my mind. It was as if I was a five-year-old kindergartener again, and the lessons from the past twenty years had never happened.

Pastor listened then asked, "Did you see her? Were you there?"

"No, but I've always felt guilty for not going home that day."

The real secret. Dear God, now he knew, too. I wanted to run.

Pastor responded immediately. "Guilt distracts us from doing good. It drowns us in self-centeredness, pity, and worry." Ah yes, self-centeredness, pity, and worry—the nurses who comfort me. Guilt is who I am, the house where I choose to live.

I didn't take in much after that, though in time I would recall Pastor's words.

"The world is chaotic, not something we can control. Order is fragile and temporary. We humans have a hard time dealing with that reality. It's too heavy a burden for us to carry by ourselves. We have to forgive and ask for forgiveness."

He paused then asked, "Shall we go pray in the sanctuary?"

We knelt before the altar. I'd never prayed out loud before, not by myself in front of strangers. So, I mumbled something about being grateful while Pastor Tim prayed about grace and redemption, about which I knew almost nothing.

As I rose to my feet, I thanked Pastor for his time and walked out of the building. I felt drained, both humiliated and humbled. Both sinner and saint.

Some might describe my "fall" in Pastor's office as a born-again experience, what Richard Rohr calls the first "dark night of the senses," when we face our unvarnished selves. For me, crossing into that liminal space was nothing short of a declaration of war—my masked "doing self" and my true "being self" positioned on opposite sides. The fall, foreshadowed while reading Gretchen's journals at Blackwater Falls, now went devastatingly public.

Part III: Finding Grace

First there is the fall, and then we recover from the fall. Both are the mercy of God.
-Lady Julian of Norwich as quoted in
Richard Rohr's *Falling Upward*

Chapter 31

At War

A week after my appointment with the pastor, I blogged about the experience—in an intellectual way. That I could do. "Am I serious about faith?" I asked again. "Can I understand myself as a sinner rather than good as I've thought all my life? Can I humble myself? Can I embrace the tension? Can I make the paradigm shift? Can I cross the line in the sand?"

Yes, I decided after clicking "Publish." I can win this war; I can pass this test. All by myself. I just need to put one foot in front of the other. So, Keith and I attended the Basics and Beginnings classes on Sunday afternoons, I took notes, and the folding chairs in the Fellowship Hall pressed cold, hard discomfort down my spine.

In *Falling Upward*, Richard Rohr defines the "shadow" or false self as an identity that emerges early in our lives. The masked self needs to look good from the outside and hide evidence to the contrary. With maturation, we learn to control our thoughts and feelings so well we don't see how self-serving they are. To enter the next stage of spiritual development, the ego must pass through a major defeat, as mine did with divorce. Thereafter I was content in the knowledge of God's love and the Spirit's guidance, until I saw my mask for what it was. During the fall and resulting war between my false and true selves, what Rohr calls "shadow boxing," I was tempted to run back to previous identities—childhood, adolescence, the false safety of intellect—whenever I perceived a threat to my basic needs of security, power, or control.

Obviously, I needed help with these temptations, but again praying never occurred to me. My masked self refused to yield to the oneness with God my true self sought. For weeks, I woke in the middle of the night soaked in sweat, teeth clenched, knees and arms pulled to chest, fists balled so tight that my fingernails dug into the palms of my hands. During the day, my GI system convulsed as if I, like the dogs, had eaten carrion resulting in an infected gut.

Doctors found no physical cause for these symptoms. Their diagnosis: GAD, generalized anxiety disorder. My poisonous demon had a name. The doctors recommended I confront anxiety head-on without medication, and I concurred. Five years later, when I realized anxiety impacted my intimacy with Keith, we'd reverse that decision. But at the time, memories of my drug-fueled breakdown in college dissuaded me. I wanted no more cover-ups. No more secrets.

What would an honest life be like, I wondered? "Walking in the light," as John describes in his Gospel. Bringing to light anxiety's poison-fueled demon of shame and shame's first cousin, the angry beast of guilt I hide behind a wall of complaints.

Anxiety. I felt relieved to be able to speak the word out loud and know what I was dealing with. Part of me had long suspected—the self who recognizes truth when it comes to light, the person who knows her anxiety is a disorder, both physical and spiritual. But the other part of me—my old familiar doing self—was convinced I'd dodged the bullet. Not me, I said with pride, I don't have Mother's anxiety because I say so. And if I don't talk about it, my anxiety will not be true.

There was the crux of the battle: confronting imperfections versus hiding them. And so, the war between my split selves—old and new, doing and being, false and true, sinner and saint—raged on.

In October, I visited Jessica in New York City. She had purchased tickets to a production of Tennessee Williams's *The Glass Menagerie*. That evening, after we found our seats in the second-row orchestra, I overheard a woman, seated to my right, regaling others about her grade-school-aged son who was sitting next to her.

"He's been acting for years." The mother glowed with pride. "He wants to be an actor. A famous actor." I saw the sliver in her eye and the log in mine. Glancing at Jessica, I wondered if she had seen my log, too.

The houselights dimmed, and we time-traveled back to a small St. Louis apartment in the 1930s. Tom, the narrator, stepped to the front of the stage and spoke. "This play is memory." As the characters came into the light on stage, my old self faded, and I watched the play with new-self eyes. I saw myself in Tom, looking at his past family with nostalgia, guilt, remorse, frustration, anger, and love. I saw myself in Amanda, a single parent, trumpeting her glory days while doing whatever she could to pay the bills: nagging, worrying, yelling, crying, laughing, making a fool of herself as I had. I saw myself in Laura, shy, crippled, and fearful, choosing distance and living in her fantasy world of blown-glass animals. I saw myself in the gentleman caller, polite, encouraging, on stage for a brief time to play the role of teacher.

    I glanced at Jessica again. Did she see herself or me in the characters? Maybe it was time for me to by-pass the play as secondary source and tell her the truth.

The next afternoon, we walked along a busy New York City street on our way to an art museum. I put my hand on her arm and blurted, "I have anxiety." I am my mother's daughter, saying things out of nowhere.

    Without missing a step, Jessica faced me and said, "Well duh, Mom. So, do I."

    My heart sank. She, too, was her mother's daughter. Like my mother, I'd worked hard not to have anxiety and even harder not to pass the disorder along, as if I could control that, too. Both of my selves lamented and for the moment called a truce.

    As we walked along, I rubbed Jessica's arm, light fingernails up and down, the way she liked me to when she was younger. What to say to show her how much I love her?

    "Oh, Sweetheart, I am so sorry. What happened? When?"

    Jessica stared straight ahead, perhaps thinking she could outdistance the truth as I had thought. "It was a while ago. The morning of the New York bar exam, I had a panic attack. I was able to talk myself down but almost didn't make it."

    I wrapped my arm around her shoulders. "But you made it, and I'm proud of you." Like mother, like daughter. Fellow strugglers—and we'd both made it.

    Jessica looked at me and smiled. "Thanks, Mom."

    We entered the lobby of the art museum. Though I'd taken a step forward, the "more" I needed to say waited. I didn't trust my old self, and my new self didn't have the words yet.

Shining light on my anxiety made it harder to hide and contain. Insomnia plagued me. I'd wake up in the wee hours and lie in bed, teetering on the edge of panic. Instead of battling the symptoms with clenched fists, fingernails, and sheer will power, I opened my palms and prayed. I remembered the Irving Berlin song Keith sang to me during our courtship and David sang for our wedding: "When I'm worried, and I can't sleep, I count my blessings instead of sheep." And I'd fall asleep—after an hour or two in open-palmed prayer—counting my blessings.

In church, I held Keith's hand during the part of the service when we confessed our sins: "I, a poor sinner, plead guilty before God of all sins. I have lived as if God did not matter and as if I mattered most. I have not honored my Lord's name as I should; my worship and prayers have faltered. I have not let His love have its way with me, and so my love for others has failed…" Later, Keith said he thought I was being sweet when I reached for his hand. I told him I was terrified and needed his support. The "being" self who lived in the light prayed with palms up. But the "doing" self still prayed with fisted hands and gritted teeth. And the word "sinner" stuck in my throat. Nope, uh-uh, not me. I'm good and right and strong.

One Sunday morning in late fall, I stood with Keith in front of the congregation and repeated the profession of faith required for church membership, my body rigid while saying the words I wanted to believe. Muscles tighter, tighter, tighter. I heard the demon's voice roiling in my gut: "You're a fraud and you know it," echoing my first panic attack. I reached for Keith's hand again to steady my pounding heart and wobbling knees.

To avoid another panic attack—in front of the entire church, no less—I moved from my gut into my head and thought about the questions intellectually, as my father had taught me. Think, Carole, think. Would I be willing to give up my life for Christ? I wanted the answer to be yes. Absolutely yes. But deep down I worried the answer wasn't so simple, and deeper down I feared the answer might be maybe. Or no. Hardly spiritual, though I wished otherwise. Or maybe that's exactly what the experience was—the same doubt I experienced at the beginning of my journey with Gretchen and her question about trust. A trust test.

Don't trust anyone, not even yourself, my inner judge said. Put one foot in front of the other, my old "doing" self said as Keith and I walked hand-in-hand back to the pew. Practice opening your heart, my new "being" self said. God is patient and trustworthy; the Spirit will guide you into the heart. Falling short of perfection is human. Keep going. But my old self had the last word: ignore your fears and gut your way through as you've always done.

And so, I did. Doing while doubting I'd ever become a "being" person.

Before Christmas, a church member who also lived in the Rockfish Valley invited me to a local women's Bible study group. The lessons filled me with hunger for the knowledge and wisdom found in scripture, the New Testament in particular. I offered to keep the roster—to serve the group and learn the women's names—and took detailed notes for my own edification. At church, I attended women's ministry activities and was asked to serve on the team. Sharing my gifts. In truth, I felt ill at ease, out of my element, and guarded. I didn't know what to do or how to "be."

In some ways, these groups were like Al-Anon, supportive communities growing and encouraging better ways to love. Less me, more Jesus. Not that I understood what that meant. Yet, sitting with the women in Bible study and church, the thought occurred to me again that I wasn't experiencing a third stage of life career change but a total reinvention. My first half of life self was dying so a truer, less selfish person could be resurrected. Gretchen had been right after all. *If you tell the truth, you're dead.* I now perceived her ominous warning as gift.

Truth-telling and dying to self. Blessings to practice. Starting with Mother.

Chapter 32

Selfies

Mother parked her walker beside the blue-cushioned booth in the Bistro dining area, set the walker brakes, and eased into the booth. She wore deep purple corduroy slacks with a matching white and purple flowered turtleneck, an attractive and serviceable ensemble for a woman in her tenth decade of life. For me, low-heeled boots, black jeans, forest-green turtleneck, and a plaid over-shirt to disguise my thickened, post-menopausal waist. Covering this unattractive quality didn't hide the truth—I wasn't fooling anyone.

In the assisted living unit where Mother lived, the staff fetched her for activities and meals. "I always go the wrong way," she'd say with a giggle. Her memory had settled into grooves like a scratched record skipping back to familiar refrains.

"Oh... I didn't know you were coming," she said when I'd arrived at my usual time. "So good to see you." After hugs and kisses, she fingered my over-shirt. "I like your shirt."

"Thank you, Mother."

She paused two beats. "I like your shirt."

"Yes, thank you, Mother. Did you go to the activity this morning?"

"Maybe. I don't remember." Giggle, beat, beat. "I like your shirt."

"Yes, thank you, Mother." I resisted the urge to roll my eyes—or cry.

She played that melodic passage four or five times, and so did I. Then her brain hopped to the next groove. "What's the news?"

At the Bistro, we sat across from one another and chatted about "the news" while nibbling the standard lunch fare: soup, sandwich, and potato-wedge fries. Residents wheeled or shuffled by, waving hello. A man and his wife stopped at our table to visit.

"This is my middle daughter," Mother said.

"Carole," I added. "Pleased to meet you."

After they were out of hearing range, Mother lowered her voice. "We play bingo together, but I don't remember their names."

Did she remember mine?

We covered "the news" again—her grandchildren, old friends, and family who might have called since my last visit. Mother asked about our dogs, Heathcliff and "the other one."

"Freya," I said.

"Oh yes." Was I prompting Mother for her benefit or mine?

We splurged on lemon meringue pie for dessert. At meal's end, she stirred her milk-laced decaf. I sipped unsweetened iced tea.

"How's the writing going?" she asked.

She remembered. At that moment, I was a teenager again, sitting at the dining room table of my childhood home with Mother drinking her decaf and me with a Coke. Ever a good listener, Mother sat still, her eyes locked on my face while I eagerly answered her question.

"Well, the manuscript needs to be simplified, refocused, more structurally consistent, so I'm putting this project on the shelf for a while. In the meantime, I'm working on an essay, taking classes, and keeping up with blog posts." I talked for several minutes.

When I finished, Mother folded her hands on the table. "I wish you well," she said. I beamed with pleasure, basking in her attention even though I knew she wouldn't remember our conversation or my visit.

After her move, Mother struggled to adjust to her new living situation. I felt helpless and estranged. Mother lasted less than a year in her apartment before anxiety consumed her. After a stint in rehab to adjust her medication, she moved to a room in a smaller assisted living unit. Now when I visited Mother, new worries coiled around old wants, creating a wound. I'd drive home after my monthly visits, down a stiff drink, talk to Keith about Mother, and weep.

Later that winter, after months of listening to my tearful recitals about her decline, Keith said to me at dinner one night, "I guess that wound is never going to heal."

"I wish she was here with me." As soon as I spoke, the thick stew, simmering on my back burner since Mother's move, boiled over.

"Just this once, I wanted Mother's love and attention." I pounded the table and wailed. "I wanted her to choose me. I wanted to win." Just this once, I wanted all the toys in the toybox. Just this once, I wanted to rescue Mother from the plane crash in our front yard, to protect her from Carl Wilson. Just this once, I wanted to be the prodigal son's older brother—the good son, the dutiful one. Instead, I'd discovered his pride and jealousy—my second lesson from the parable.

My hand shot up, too late to cover the words that had escaped my mouth. That past was not past either. Keith stared at me. "Oh, Carole, you need to pray God takes that from your heart."

The hand over my mouth dropped. "I had no idea."

As soon as I said those words, my eyes widened. That was a lie, and I knew it. My needy, winner-takes-all self-centeredness snapped into the light. No more denying. No more hiding. No more running from the past.

I stared back to Keith. "I guess it's time to put my childish ways behind me."

In the days that followed I prayed palms-up for guidance. Then I set a goal: to visit Mother in her present and be the adult daughter she needed me to be. The changes in me didn't happen overnight—I backslid many times—nor did the changes in Mother.

The following month, I noticed Jane had labeled Mother's bureau drawers with post-it notes—Underwear. Socks. Tops. Pants. Sweaters. Laptop—and laid out clothes on her bed, matching pants and tops. Since cataract surgery, Mother talked about colors more often. She didn't use the computer by herself anymore. Younger friends and family emailed messages and pictures, some of which Mother wanted to print so she could keep them in the basket beside her reclining chair.

To help her remember "the news," I'd purchased a simple inkjet color printer. During my visit, I connected the printer to Mother's old laptop. Then I snuggled next to her and held my iPhone at arm's length.

"Ready? Hold still." I took a selfie of the two of us then tapped the image. Mother's expression was relaxed, mine stiff and open-mouthed.

I took a few more mother-daughter selfies then sent the best image to Mother's email and printed. "Oh, my soul." Mother chuckled when I handed her the print. "Isn't that something?"

While we studied the picture, I stared at myself, wishing I'd worn a bright-colored top, combed my hair, put on lipstick, didn't look so clueless. I eased into the Hitchcock rocker across from Mother. Phooey on my selfish selfies, Mother's delight was all that mattered.

After our three-hour visit together, Mother wheeled her walker down the hall to the exit. We embraced and kissed goodbye. I inhaled. She smelled clean. If I couldn't do for her every day, at least I could make sure she was well tended. Tender mercy for her.

"Drive safely," she said.

"Take good care, Mother. I'll email you when I get home. Jane will read my message to you tonight."

"I look forward to it. I love you."

"I love you, too."

That night, Keith and I went to dinner at a local Italian restaurant. After the salad course was served, he asked about Mother.

"We had a good visit." I sipped a large glass of Chianti. For the first time since Mother's move, I spoke about her situation without weeping. "I think she enjoyed our selfie. Maybe she'll remember my visit, maybe she won't." I averted my eyes.

Keith reached across the table and took my hand. "It's okay to want that for yourself, Carole. It's not selfish."

I remembered my greed the day after Mother got hurt, when I fell on the newly shellacked floor in my parents' bedroom, where my mother had almost bled to death. But instead of allowance money for sweets, I had wanted Mother's sweetness. And it was okay to want that for myself.

Tender mercy for me. Another step forward.

Chapter 33

Trust Tests

Life flowed from spring into summer. I visited Mother, took classes at Writer House in Charlottesville, and joined a critique group. Keith and I hosted family and friends, stockpiled firewood, and attended church—me still doing while doubting. Though I felt I'd made progress with Jessica and Mother, the war between my two selves was far from over. I would have another opportunity to learn more about grace and mercy, this time with Freya.

One clear Sunday evening in August, I opened the kitchen door to let her inside. Instead of bounding across the great room to one of the nest beds, she slunk to our bedroom closet, the place where she hid during thunderstorms. She whimpered when I sat down beside her.

"What's wrong, girl?" Saliva and blood dripped from her mouth. Though lethargic, she breathed at twice her normal rate and panted.

I called up to Keith in the loft. "Freya's hurt. She's bleeding and crying in our closet."

Keith came downstairs immediately. He stroked his hands over her body, checking for injuries. Freya's muzzle and throat were swollen. I removed her collar to ease her breathing.

"Let's see if she'll eat a piece of cheese," Keith said. "If she does, then she's probably all right." When he held the cheese up to her nose, Freya touched then refused the treat. I called the vet and explained the situation. He said she needed twenty-four-hour care only available at the emergency animal hospital in Charlottesville.

I grabbed my purse and car keys. "Go in the car?" Heathcliff scrambled down the stairs and into the garage, followed more slowly by Freya. When Keith opened the Subaru's hatch, Heathcliff leaped into the back.

"Come on, baby girl," I said to Freya. She managed the jump without assistance. Keith sat in the passenger seat, and Freya rested her head on the console between us.

We rode in silence, tense and lost in thought. I remembered when Jessica was a baby, and my first husband and I took her to the emergency room. Though we'd given her the prescribed antibiotic for an ear infection, she'd spiked a fever late in the afternoon. From 101 to 102 to 103. At 104, I stripped her clothes off and bathed her in a tub of cool water. When the fever hit 105, we loaded Jessica into her car seat and headed to Medical City Dallas Hospital.

Jess was their only patient that evening, so the emergency room doctors gave her plenty of attention. She wailed during the examination and tests. I wanted to wrap my arms around my baby and rock her, lightly rubbing up and down her soft skin, soothing and protecting her from the pain in life. It seemed an eternity before the doctors and nurses handed her back to me.

While we waited for results, Jess toddled around the waiting room, her baby blonde wisps curling at the nape of her neck. The doctors said all was well. Jess's fever had broken, and her temperature returned to normal. Had I overreacted? Would Jessica have recovered if I'd just stayed the course?

Was I overreacting now? Would Freya recover on her own, without putting her through this intrusion? Given the extent of Freya's neck and facial swelling, like a soccer ball on the side of her neck, we thought not.

The emergency hospital vet diagnosed a snakebite. She told us the clinic treated several cases each day this time of year and showed us the puncture wounds in Freya's lower lip. Freya's treatment included IV fluids, antibiotics, pain medication, and an overnight stay. Throughout the night, they would monitor her blood pressure and watch for signs of internal bleeding. Allergic reaction to snake venom can lead to difficulty clotting blood, we learned, and the first twenty-four hours are critical.

Heathcliff whined and worried when we left the hospital without Freya. But at home, he settled into his nest bed in the great room as usual. I slept fitfully.

Over 5 a.m. coffee the next morning, Keith and I agreed to a division of labor. Since he has a fondness for snakes—I do not—he donned heavy work gloves and cleaned around the woodpile where we thought Freya had run afoul of a copperhead. He also took care of Heathcliff while I tended to Freya.

I drove into town, my brain fogged from lack of sleep, mirroring the early-morning fog, which blanketed the Rockfish Valley. *Please, please help Freya-dog*, I prayed, doing my best to hold mind, heart, and body together, to stay calm, open, and connected. As the vet briefed me, I wrote down the information, asked questions, and noted clarifications, making sure I had everything straight.

"Snake bites are quite painful for humans and dogs," she said. "Smaller dogs can die if they get a large dose of venom. Larger dogs have a better chance but need to be monitored."

I paid the bill while the vet tech led Freya into the lobby. Freya was stoic and obedient, accepting of the IV taped to her leg. She looked at me, muzzle down, eyes up. Her Princess Di look. After climbing into the back of the Subaru, she propped her head on the console and nudged my arm for gentle head stroking.

"Good girl, Freya, good girl." I cooed and massaged her head the way she liked. "We'll take good care of you, baby girl." I delivered her to our regular vet so they could monitor blood-clotting rates and continue treatment for the next twelve hours.

Driving back to Vanaprastha, I noticed the fog had lifted from all except Afton Mountain. Sometimes mountain-top wisdom comes in a cloud if we ask and wait and trust in God's love. I recalled the scripture from 1 Corinthians chapter 13, which Jessica read at our wedding. *Love is patient, love is kind. It does not envy, it does not boast, it is not proud. It is not rude, it is not self-seeking, it is not easily angered, it keeps no record of wrongs. Love does not delight in evil but rejoices with the truth. It always protects, always trusts, always hopes, always perseveres. Love never fails.* God's love is perfect—patient, kind, truthful, protective, trusting, hopeful, consistent—but mine is not. My less-than-perfect love often falls short due to envy, pride, anger, jealousy, grudge, and lack of trust. Yet, in the fog and clouds atop Afton Mountain, I sensed the grace of God and the Spirit's challenge for me to raise the bar, to learn how to "be" in my heart.

Later that afternoon, I returned to pick up Freya. The vet handed me antibiotics—twice-a-day with meals—and pain medication, every four hours. Before bedtime at 9 p.m., I offered Freya a pain pill wrapped in liverwurst. She took the treat obediently but not with her usual enthusiasm.

Instead of sleeping by the window near Keith, Freya lay on the floor at the foot of our bed. I woke at 2 a.m. to the sound of her whimpering and crying. As I had many times with my children when they were growing up, I slipped out of bed and tended to her.

"It's okay, Freya, it's okay, baby girl." I held another liverwurst-wrapped pain pill to her nose. "Eat this, and you'll feel better." She licked the pill out of the palm of my hand. I stayed by her side with my hand on her soft belly until her breathing calmed and she slept.

The 2 a.m. waking and pill dosage routine lasted for the next few nights. Within a week, Freya returned to her usual playful self. But our relationship had changed—some.

We had been tested. Freya showed me her vulnerability and offered trust, and, in my own way, I had done the same. I suppose in the past my "doing" self would have felt a sense of pride, convinced I had saved Freya—I'd finally rescued someone. But I knew Keith would always be her savior; she would sleep beside him and seek his affection. And I would love her without expecting anything in return. Freya was getting the care she needed—like Mother. That's all that mattered. Unlike my "doing" self's jealousy, my "being" self could love joyfully.

Jessica, Mother, Freya. A third step forward.

Chapter 34

Steps Forward and Back

Perhaps because of my success with Freya, I felt confident enough to write the scene of my panic attack in Pastor's office—a full year later. I reentered the time and place, replayed the devastating fall in mind and body, and recreated dialogue, physical actions, and responses. When I thought I'd captured the scene accurately, I emailed the draft to Pastor Tim.

"Would you please read the attached and make corrections and suggestions?" I wrote in my email. "I want to get the theology correct. Thank you so much for your guidance."

A month went by, during which my writing group critiqued the draft and gave me favorable feedback. But I knew something was off. I requested another meeting with Pastor.

This time we sat across from one another at the small meeting table in his office.

He paged through the printout. "I really like what you wrote." While he pointed out sections he found particularly effective, I took notes and beamed with pleasure.

Then he shifted in his chair and waited until I looked up. "You forgot God's mercy, you forgot forgiveness." In the draft I had sent to him, everything after his comment about guilt, distracting us from doing good, and my thought—guilt is who I am—was missing.

I blinked in surprise. Forgiveness? How could I forget forgiveness? Didn't Pastor always say, "As His servant and as your Pastor, I announce the Father's forgiveness to you," at the end of confession? Confessing Our Sin & Receiving Forgiveness—part of every worship service. So, why did the words "sin and forgiveness" still catch in my throat?

One big step back.

When we knelt at the altar after our second meeting, I mumbled again. I still felt exposed, too frightened to pray out loud, fearing I'd make a mistake. Or reveal too much.

After leaving the sanctuary, I squared my shoulders and asked myself what. What did I not want to reveal? I decided to practice praying out loud, hoping to discover the What.

Seated across the dinner table from Keith that night, I said, "I'd like to say grace from now on, if you don't mind." He extended his hand and bowed his head. Silence. I took his right hand in my left, opened my right hand palm up, bowed my head, and prayed. Out loud.

"Dear Lord, thank you for this day, for the beauty of your creation… we are in awe." An easy place to begin. Then my brain struggled to find words. I glanced up at Keith's bowed head. Love. "Thank you for loving us, for bringing Keith and me together, for the love that we share." Widen the circle. "Thank you for our family, friends, and neighbors. Please watch over all of us, especially our children and the little ones." Then words borrowed from Keith. "Thank you for the missions you've given us and the skills to accomplish them. Please guide us on your path." Standard finish spoken in a heart-pounding rush. "And we ask that you bless this food we're about to receive. In the name of your Son Jesus. Amen."

A big step forward.

One Sunday morning after the New Year, the order of worship in church included the sacrament of infant baptism. The infant: a baby girl. Baptism: a visible sign of an invisible grace.

"I was there to hear your borning cry, I'll be there when you are old," we sang at the beginning of the ceremony. "I rejoiced the day you were baptized, to see your life unfold."

Pastor Tim held the baby, cupped his hand into the baptismal font, and bathed her forehead with water. Tears welled in my eyes. "Welcome to your new family of Christians," Pastor said, carrying the baby down the aisle.

Family of Christians—not my birth family. How much had I missed? I could not stop the flow of tears down my cheeks. Grabbing a tissue from my purse, I dabbed my eyes, hoping I didn't look like a mascara-smeared raccoon.

As we were leaving the sanctuary and heading to our car, I turned to Keith. "I was so embarrassed during the baptism. Did you see me crying?"

"Yes, were you crying for the baby or yourself?" Discerning as usual—what I counted on. Yet I felt snake bit.

My shoulders slumped, and I sighed. "Myself, I guess."

A giant step back.

Okay, I said to myself, I'm being childish again, mourning lost time and feeling sad for what my parents didn't do for me. They gave me their best. Isn't that enough?

Driving home from church, I thought about my first meeting with Pastor, my 'checked box' baptism. "People come to church for many reasons," he'd said. "It's not for me to judge."

So, I got baptized for the wrong reason. It's not for me or anyone to judge. I'm here now, trying to find my way to the light, and that's all that matters to God.

One baby step forward.

A year and a half after Keith and I joined the church, I was still doing while doubting, particularly during Communion. When I followed Keith up the aisle to receive bread and wine, the body and blood of Jesus really present, I felt self-conscious. An unworthy party-crasher, a fraud, afraid of making a mistake or doing something stupid. Sitting by myself and watching others receive Communion had been easier. Part of me preferred the separateness, the safety of distance, detachment, and self-pity, rather than step to the altar and connect to suffering and joy. The other part of me knew that knocking down those walls and moving toward common union with others was essential for redemption and freedom, healing, and peace.

I figured the finding was only a matter of time and practice. As C.S. Lewis wrote in *Mere Christianity*, "Very often the only way to get a quality in reality is to start behaving as if you had it already." Like a child donning her parents' clothes and pretending to be an adult, or a college student dressing like a teacher to become one. Building a new heart, new muscles, new memories. Bread and wine taken in by faith.

But no matter what clothes I wore or how I pretended to be a faithful adult, my father's words often accompanied me up the aisle during Communion. "This is a bunch of hooey," I'd hear inside my head—what I had heard him say while growing up. Each time I heard those rebellious words, my old self ignored them and put one foot in front of the other. As usual.

One Sunday, maybe Eastertime, the words followed me to the altar again. This time I prayed. *Help me, Lord, I don't want to hear this voice anymore.* Immediately, inside my head, I heard myself say, "Be quiet, Daddy, you are not my god. You had your journey. This is between me and God."

As I sat down after taking Communion, I felt like I'd graduated again from pitiful child to rebellious adolescent. The twenty-one-year-old girl inside a sixty-three-year-old woman, still angry with her tender-hearted father. And yet I knew the voice speaking in my head was not Daddy's. All the voices were mine. But from that day forward, I didn't hear that "hooey" voice anymore. We celebrate even small victories when at war.

Later, I remembered one of my father's younger brothers telling me Daddy had asked God for forgiveness and found God's peace in the days before he died. Why didn't I ask for the same? I was free to choose. And peace was what I wanted, right? So, what was holding me back?

What?

Chapter 35

Both-And Teachers

While searching for What, I visited Mother every month. I'd decided to use my teaching skills to stimulate her recall and help her remember who she was. She had been my teacher, now I would be hers. Before each visit, I designed mental lesson plans as I had with Heathcliff. Behavioral objectives, resource materials, instructional strategies: Mother will be able to view photographs of her life in old albums and tell stories; I'll point to pictures, ask questions, and wait for her responses. After summary and closure—hugs and saying our goodbyes—I'll evaluate our session during my drive home. The assessment would not be based on Mother's learning, which she couldn't do anymore, but on my ability to be the adult daughter she needed me to be.

Mother and Daddy had grown up in the same farm community in northern Maine. Every summer and winter, we visited the folks back home. As a child, I paid little attention to Mother's oft-told tales from her youth. Now I craved her stories, because they primed her memory, deepened my understanding of our past, and gave us something to talk about.

One day, during lunch at the Bistro, I asked, "Did you and your mother talk when you were growing up?"

"No." Mother smirked, her familiar wry smile.

"Did your parents talk to each other?"

"Not much." Mother stretched the o and u vowels into "ahs" like a Downeast Mainer.

I chuckled. She was making me work. "When they did, what did they talk about?"

"The weather." Mother laughed out loud. "We listened to the radio in the living room, but the kitchen was where everything happened. In winter, we moved the dining room table into the kitchen near the stove and did our homework or played Rook in the evenings. My mother did needlework." Grammy, a woman who knitted her love into our socks and mittens.

Mother was still talking as we rode the elevator back to her main-floor room. "I remember when my mother got her washing machine. She polished it all up, really babied it. It saved her a lot of time. She'd start it, and we'd hear *Put-Put-Put-Put-Put*."

As we rolled past the nurses' station in the lobby, Mother's story teetered on the edge of an old memory groove. "My mother only got an eighth-grade education but always wanted to be a doctor. She would've been a good one."

I tensed, anticipating one of her bad-day, oft-told kitchen-table-talks, which went like this: "I had to fight for everything I got, including an education. My mother backed me on that. Dad grudgingly paid my tuition so I could become a teacher but said it was a waste of money."

Today, that past got lost, but mine didn't. Daddy, questioning me about tuition insurance. How long was I going to hang onto that old story? How long until I could leave it? In truth, I'd exhibited plenty of prodigal behavior to worry my parents; in faith, an atheist could not be more disobedient. What would I have seen if I'd looked at myself through their eyes? I thought I could off-set my transgressions by denying or hiding them and earning love, especially Father Abraham's. And where did earning love lead me? To exhaustion, a breakdown, and years of resentment. As the saying goes, holding a grudge is like drinking poison and expecting the other person to die. Though I'd wanted to die, I hadn't wanted to kill myself, and I hadn't wanted my father to die. Ever. I only wanted his love, like God's love: steadfast, always, forever.

As Mother rolled into her room and settled in her reclining chair, I thought about the misunderstandings, missteps, mistakes, and disappointments we experience in life. All were opportunities for me to learn and grow as a person of faith. But only if I stopped drinking poison.

An arrangement of mini pink carnations on the windowsill scented the room. Thanks to Jane, Mother always had fresh-cut flowers. I handed Mother the old scrapbook. She opened the cover and ran her hands over the faded grey construction paper.

"There's Mother and Dad. Paul, Arlene, Mansfield, and me." She pointed to the corner-mounted pictures. "And my classmates at normal school in Presque Isle. I wonder if any of them are still alive." Mother had outlived her siblings, her husband, and most of her friends. "Our dorm was near the airfield," she said, referring to the World War II military base. "From the window of my room, I could see the pilots in their cockpits, taking off. We signed up for shifts to identify planes. I had…" Mother formed cylinders with her fingers and raised them to her eyes.

"Binoculars for reconnaissance?"

"Yes, binoculars. I also worked blackout patrol. I drove around after dark and beeped my horn for people to turn off their house lights."

She turned the page. "My students and the schoolhouse." She pointed to class pictures taken outside the building. "I taught K-4 in the room to the left, and the other teacher had grades 5-8 in the room on the right. 1943-46—I started when I was twenty."

"Oh my, you were young, Mother." About the same age as I was when student-teaching history to high school students. "And here's your wedding picture."

"Your father was still in uniform, November 1945." Mother paused. "Three times your father was assigned to units and transferred before he reached the front. Those units were wiped out to a man, three times." She held up three fingers.

"I guess Daddy was meant to survive." I hoped my often-repeated comments to familiar stories would keep her going, remembering stories prompted by pictures in the album. "Is that Jack?" Jack was Mother's childhood dog.

"Yes, Jack at home with me before your father and I moved to the University of Maine."

"What happened to Jack?"

"Oh, that's painful." Mother's child voice. I waited, hoping she would find the courage to face the memory. This time she did. "Dad died soon after your sister Jane was born, and the farm was sold. Jack was old. My family didn't think he'd adjust to the move. So, they took him out and shot him."

"I'm so sorry about Jack, Mother. I guess that's what people did back then." As Mother and I looked at more photographs, I thought of Heathcliff and Freya, waiting for me at home. How would I handle their deaths, or Mother's, my sisters' or friends', my children's, Keith's, or my own? More to the point, how was I handling the life I'd been given?

Later, Mother walked with me down the hall to the lobby. "Drive safely," she said.

"Take care, Mother. I'll email you when I get home."

I waited for her to say, "I love you." But she didn't, so I spoke first.

"I love you, too," she said. As we hugged, I kissed her goodbye. Clean.

On the drive home, I recalled an expression Mother had said for many years after retiring from teaching in her early seventies: "The day I stop learning, just shoot me." I shuddered. Like Jack, who her family thought couldn't learn anymore. Like my mother.

Two months later, Mother paged through the album with me again, pointing at pictures, naming the people, places, and events. She peered at the photographs more deliberately, having been diagnosed with macular degeneration. Thankfully, Mother repeated almost everything she'd told me previous times. Past memories seemed intact although shorter.

"There's your father, still in uniform at our wedding. Three times he was assigned to units then transferred, and those units were wiped out, three times." Three fingers. "And there's Jack before your father and I moved to the University."

Walking to the lobby at the end of our visit, Mother asked, "Your father studied what?"

"Engineering before and during the war then he switched to medicine."

"Oh yes, that's right, the GI Bill. Your father always wanted to be a doctor." She paused then found an old wound. "I remember my dad sitting at the dining room table back home, shaking his head and saying, 'He'll never do it. He'll never become a doctor.'"

"And you and Daddy showed him, didn't you?"

"Yes, we showed him." Mother beamed with pleasure.

I hugged and kissed her. "Take care, Mother, I'll email you when I get home. I love you."

Mother did not respond. I caught the eye of an aide, sitting at the nurses' station across from the exit. She nodded.

Driving home, I assessed the visit. With fading eyesight and memory, eventually Mother would not be able to see the photographs or answer questions. I would have to revise my objective: to abide with Mother in her present and let the past go.

Then I thought about what I'd said, how Mother and Daddy showed her father. Had I shown mine? I supposed I had, though the honors were hardly satisfying, because I had forgotten forgiveness. Apparently, I would have to learn the forgiveness lesson again and again and again.

Heart-centered practice. By caring for one parent, my relationship with the other parent was shifting. *Thanks to Dad in a special way—* Gretchen's childhood words.

My grip relaxed on the steering wheel. I recalled what I'd told my students at the end of student teaching: "I hope you learned at least a fraction of what you taught me." I hoped my visits benefited Mother at least a fraction of how they benefited me.

She was teaching me to love the past for what was and the present for what it is.

Chapter 36

Gretchen's Goodbye

September 23, 2015. The Autumnal Equinox. Gretchen's thirty-ninth birthday. I sat at my desk on the main floor at Vanaprastha, and Keith directly above me at his desk in the loft. He was quiet, as he was on every birthday since her death. Not sad but remembering. Maybe he thought about the day he brought Penny home or about taking Gretchen to the library, museums, the aquarium, camping, shopping, or giving her birthday and Christmas presents, sharing his curiosity. Golden memories of her smile, her laugh, her childhood lisp, her clever wit and insight when older.

He said he thought about her every day, mostly happy thoughts now. But when Keith and I first met, less than two years after her death, grief still caught him by surprise. One morning in church, we sang the hymn, "Go, My Children, With My Blessing," to the same tune as the lullaby, "All Through the Night."

Go, my children, with my blessing; Never alone.
Waking, sleeping, I am with you; You are my own.

Suddenly I couldn't hear Keith's baritone voice. I glanced sideways and saw tears coursing down his face. I handed him a tissue and covered his other hand with mine.

"Damn." He muttered under his breath. "I wish I hadn't picked my favorite hymns for Gretchen's memorial service. Now I can't sing them anymore."

Damn, I said to myself, I wish I wasn't angry with her. I hate the trouble she caused. I hate this suffering. I hate that she killed herself and caused him this pain.

What terrible thoughts, and in church no less. I bowed my head in shame.

Now on Gretchen's birthday, sitting at my desk with her last journal in hand, I realized I had been angry with Gretchen even before reading her journals that first time. Anger and blame were safer than love's Both-And tension. I had chosen the easier path. But I wasn't angry with her anymore, not after what we'd been through. Maybe someday I wouldn't be angry with myself for wanting to be right and in control, for being too afraid to love and too stiff-necked to forgive. Maybe someday I'd stop wishing I'd been there to save Gretchen, which spoke to my delusion, not hers. I would have failed to be what she needed me to be, as my father failed me, as I failed Jessica. Truth be told, I failed to love my first husband well, too. We all fail one another because we are not perfect like God. Wanting to be perfect and avoid suffering were the reasons I'd hidden my failures and hard times in a closet.

Keith didn't block memories of his suffering—that would have been counter to his confrontational nature. Yet I doubted he lingered on those difficult years. That would be counter to his optimism. I, on the other hand, needed to accept the truth, to sit uncomfortably in that chair. To widen my brain's aperture to see both the sinner and the saint in Gretchen and me. To read her last entry one more time and face the hardest time of all.

* * *

June 22, 2001: "My grandmother [Keith's mother] phoned this morning. It's very odd, she has always, in the past, contacted me with almost a psychic inevitability whenever I was in straits. I reassured her. Nothing is the matter; I have hugely complicated future plans! It's true.

"Harry called to say that he'd be coming by; his voice carried an odd note, so I knew he'd be with company. He seemed on edge in my apartment, very tense. I went through my camera skit. I explained that when I take out my photograph album years from now, I want to have a picture and say, "This is my friend." I think myself graceful for having said this. It is he who should have this photo. He agreed very easily, because I phrased it in a way to sound rather noble instead of martyred. I am a bit proud of this, I admit.

"He set the timer on the camera. We seated ourselves in front of the lens, a moment for his future contemplation. He will wonder about this moment for a while, perhaps a long while. I took my own photograph in my head. This tiny moment erased every complication. The camera flashed. We looked at the image and laughed. He laughed tightly; I laughed with great abandon. I had been freed of my regrets and worries at that moment; it was, to me, exactly as if we were friends and always had been.

"He asked if I wanted to meet his fiancée, then, before they left. I laughed and went out to meet the partner who had replaced me in usefulness. It was interesting. I wanted to see them interact together in the way of all the wondrously synchronous pairings I've been honored to know. If only I had been in abstract consciousness divorced from my body, I might have witnessed this between them. I am only me, and for whatever reason, I was unable to receive that sense of wholeness I always allow to wash over me when I'm in its presence. I'd take it on faith that I'd be privileged to experience it in their company. I rushed up the stairs, eager to meet her. I felt like a vast multitude: a shouting, conquering army.

"We discussed random things. She mistook my name. Gretchen: tiny pearl in German, fig in Hebrew, terrible head in Gaelic. These define me—I have been a treasure to some, a first morsel of nourishment following starvation of the soul, and the victory prize, a flaunted trophy. This is my name.

"When I came inside following the climax of this whole tale, I had a sudden, tremendous desire to phone Paul to share a beer or two, to pour out my life to him like wine all over his shoulders. I did this. 'I think I'd like that beer now,' were my final, tiny words to his answering machine.

"And so, I am putting off the fulfillment of my duty. I suppose I must be afraid. I have been, of most things, so this suits me. It isn't a great hectic fear, only an uncertainty, that I may have left things undone. The way you wonder if you've forgotten to pack things for a long trip.

"These words. At last, all I have are futile words deferring my obligations. And there it is.

> *If I surrender my arms to you*
> *In the green hills of our friendship*
> *Do I live a little less*

Or will the sun burst forth clad
In the colour of lemons?
The sky has brightened over our
Heads for a million years...
How like the taste of tangerines
To think of it, to think of all the days
Scattering blue fire over the heads of those
We've loved, now gone,
And those we will love,
Not yet born
Gretchen Kenny"

* * *

I closed Gretchen's journal. From what the Alexandria police told Keith, she covered her desk with plastic and called the local police station. "Someone is going to die tonight," she said. "Please come." She gave her address—so the police would find her instead of Paul or someone else—and hung up the phone. Then she picked up a gun, released the safety, put the barrel in her mouth, and fired.

Gretchen did not die in the Alexandria townhouse, but part of Keith did. I will never forget his story. No matter how many times he told me, the recounting never changed.

At 3 a.m. on Saturday morning, he woke to a knock on his front door. When he saw two police officers standing there, he knew. Gretchen. Even though she seemed to be doing better—growing her art business, moving to a new apartment, learning to drive—the therapist had advised him years before this was a possible scenario. That's the demon of shame, the beast of sin, and the slow poison of mental illness.

He invited the police into his house. They stood together in the living room, and the officers moved right up close to him. "I'm okay," he said to them, "you don't need to stay, but I wish she'd called me."

Cold loneliness crept into his body. For a year, no matter how warmly he dressed or how hot the temperature or how many blankets he piled on, he felt the cold, lonely chill in his body, especially at night when he tried to sleep. Every day he'd see something he wanted to share with Gretchen, something she'd enjoy, then remember she was gone. But he knew relief from loss would replace sadness, eventually. With time, lonely regret would fade into those golden memories. She was her father's darling daughter—that is what he'd remember.

What had Gretchen wanted? To be worthy, Keith told me, to restore broken people and rescue simple creatures. The Saint. Yet her desire for freedom and pleasure often dictated her actions. The Sinner. In love, she wanted wholeness, a perfect love she called Merged Permanence, but would not allow others to help restore her brokenness or rescue her from destruction. Her Narrowest Margin of Victory was death. I, too, had wanted wholeness, but my actions spoke to my childish need for attention and approval. Success was my Narrowest Margin of Victory, and I was willing to kill my self— my real self—in order to earn success and win. Although our wants and needs were impossible to fulfill, failure was something Gretchen and I could not accept. Or forgive.

Gretchen scared me because her honesty exposed my dishonesty. I feared her self-destruction because I feared my own. I struck in anger, blaming those who might cause pain, and distanced myself from confrontation and intimacy. But shielding myself from suffering locked me inside a prison of aloneness, causing even more pain and preventing me from getting what my soul longed for: a healing heart.

I set Gretchen's journal aside. Seeking truth, self-knowledge, and healing are inseparably entwined, I thought, and those experiences connect us to one another. That was her gift to me, and through me, to our readers. Witnesses to the wounds that live on in us, wounds so secret we might not be aware of them, secrets brought to light by writing about them. I'd found my new mission: to use my teaching gift as a writer.

Hearing Keith roll his chair away from his desk, I mounted the stairs to the loft. "You're thinking of Gretchen today." He nodded. "I've been thinking about her, too. Do you have a copy of her memorial service?" Ask me anything. No secrets.

Keith scooted to the edge of his chair. "I can find one and email a copy of my speech to you, too, if you'd like." He opened his desk file drawer.

While flipping through file folders, he launched into the story. "After Gretchen's death, I received phone calls—everyone knew we were close. Everyone felt guilty for what happened, and Gretchen wasn't there to say they weren't responsible." He looked up at me. "That's why I had to tell them, so they wouldn't blame themselves."

After handing me the program, he set the scene. "The church was packed. I thanked everyone for coming then took off my jacket, tie, and dress shirt to reveal my Hawaiian shirt underneath." Gretchen disliked formality, he explained. Her spirit was more likely to join them if she knew he'd be speaking in church in his Hawaiian shirt. I smiled, thinking about these two contrarians.

Keith didn't need to refer to his speech—his memory of the service from fourteen years prior tracked word-for-word with the computer file he emailed to me later. "The saddest thing some say is to bury your own child. Well, God blessed me with a wonderful daughter for almost twenty-five years, and I am happy to have had her that long. The good Gretchen did should be remembered because she gave us all she had."

He told stories—tender stories, quirky stories, funny stories. "Gretchen was an easy person to love—a lot of fun, most of the time. Great to work with, and she could talk on almost anything. But she could be a pain in the butt. She was brilliant, but she was unreasonable and immature, and she didn't like to follow the rules. 'Sorry Sweetheart, you know it's true.'" I chuckled at his candor, expecting nothing less.

"And there was laughter," he said. "At a memorial for a suicide. Can you imagine?"

Harry was there with his fiancée, Keith told me. "It wasn't his fault." Keith's voice hardened. "Gretchen used him. If not him, she would have found someone else to play the role. Using him is the only thing I cannot forgive her."

He doesn't hide his anger or his suffering, I thought, yet forgiveness still challenges him even after fourteen years. Love is easy, loving is hard. Yes, he knew, he lived it, and in a small way so had I. Wrapping my arms around his weight-lifter's shoulders, I held him for a long, long time.

Later, reading the memorial service program, I jolted at Keith's choice for an opening hymn: "I Was There to Hear Your Borning Cry." Of course. Sweet Gretchen's baptism. I wrapped my arms around an imagined infant, nestled her body close to my heart—as I had my own children—and rocked her for a long, long time.

Soon after Gretchen's birthday, while pulling invasive stilt grass along the driveway, I discovered a turtle the size of a silver dollar, hiding under a mountain laurel bush. A coincidence? I cradled the turtle in the palm of my hand and called to Keith.

He checked her markings. "A female Eastern box turtle." He rubbed her soft plastron with his thumb. "Maybe one of Penny's children." He handed the turtle back to me.

"The baby turtle's chances for survival are slim," I said. "And even her adult future isn't guaranteed." My voice trailed off. I thought about the day we let Penny go and how I breathed in molecules—Gretchen's or Galileo's—and I let them go.

"It's nature's way, we are not in control," Keith said. "All we can do is hope."

I re-covered her with leaf litter. "Live long and well, little turtle. No matter what happens, you are never alone." With that, I said goodbye to Gretchen. The daughter I would never meet. A girl who'd felt unworthy of God's grace.

A woman like me.

Chapter 37

The Comfort of Guilt

Dog toenails clicked on the wood floors from the great room into our bedroom as strong gusts of wind rattled the house. I opened an eyelid and saw Heathcliff staring out our bedroom window into the moonlight. He panted and paced then click-clicked to my side of the bed. With head and muzzle, he butted my arm.

I stroked his soft ear. "Okay, boy, we'll go to the basement."

Sliding out of bed so as not to wake Keith, I slipped on my scuffs and robe, snagged the leash hanging on the French doors in the great room, and headed to the kitchen. Heathcliff dogged my steps. His bag of Composure, an herbal medication for anxiety, lay in a bin on the counter next to his arthritis pills.

At seven, Heathcliff was now middle-aged. For several months, he'd come home lame after running up and down the mountain full tilt. The vet recommended curtailed activity until he recovered and prescribed on-going arthritis medication. Then one day, Heathcliff limped up the driveway on three legs. He'd ruptured his left cranial cruciate ligament, an injury analogous to an ACL injury in humans and common in slim-hipped dogs like Heathcliff.

Our vet sent us to a large dog specialist who performed TPLO surgery, tibial-plateau-leveling osteotomy, to stabilize the joint. Rehab was time intensive. Because I was often wakeful and Keith slept through the night most of the time, I covered night duty as I had with Freya. Keith handled physical therapy exercises during the day. Partnership. Leveraging our strengths. I also added Heathcliff's progressive walks to mine. But no stair-climbing, the specialist warned.

I grabbed the bag of Composure chews and leashed Heathcliff. We made our way out the back door and down the gentle, moonlit slope to the driveway. After I punched the four-digit access code to open the garage door, we walked through the garage, crossed the basement stairwell, and entered the man cave, the quietest room in the house.

Heathcliff sat for his medication treat, which looked and smelled like a triangle of chocolate. For a moment, I thought I, too, could use a piece of composure on my bad nights. Drugs. Side effects. The temptation passed. I dimmed the overhead lights and closed the door so Heathcliff would not be tempted to climb the stairs. Then I pulled a dog bed next to the sofa.

"Heathcliff, lie down." I patted the dog bed. "Down."

I curled on the sofa and rested my hand on his belly until he stopped panting and his breathing slowed—as I had with Freya. Once he fell asleep, I slipped out of the man cave and back into bed with Keith. I hated leaving Heathcliff alone in the basement—a bad decision—but leaving Keith was worse. He always sensed my absence and patted my side of the bed, searching for me. Then he slid one leg across the empty contours of my body so he would feel my return. And I always came back, because I'm the staying type, even when I feel like running.

Heathcliff will be all right, I told myself. As I lay in bed, I wondered if my anxiety had transferred to him, given his natural sense of compassion for others, especially me. No, Heathcliff likely developed wind anxiety because his injury made him vulnerable, like Freya's snake bite.

What injury made Keith vulnerable? Gretchen.

And me? Mother's.

My answer surprised me. I'd never thought about Mother's injury as my vulnerability before, except for feeling guilty. Hadn't I given up the guilt now that I'd revealed my real secret? And forgiveness always follows confession in the order of worship, right?

I waited for one of those epiphany moments. But this time, there was no insight, no overwhelming feeling of joy and gratitude. So, I set my question aside for later and slept.

At the beginning of my sabbatical, I'd made three promises: to build a house with Keith, get to know Gretchen, and become a responsible dog-owner. Over the course of four years, my promises had changed slightly. We had built the physical mountain house and now worked on the metaphorical house: our relationship. Though I listened to Keith's stories and read Gretchen's journals in their entirety, I'd said goodbye to my foil. And I had become resigned to the fact that Heathcliff would always be a goofy, distractible, stubborn adolescent, in need of daily reinforcement for the rest of his life.

Unlike training, rehabbing Heathcliff was easy, perhaps because the slow pace and frequency of our walks gave me more God time. Another coincidence? Both of us gained confidence during those cool, October walks. Soon we were climbing stairs again—literally for him, figuratively for me.

One morning, I decided to revisit what I'd written about my panic attack in the pastor's office, searching for clues to why I'd forgotten forgiveness. Scooting back from my desk, I perched on the edge of my chair as if it was the sofa in Pastor's office, crossed my legs at the ankles, folded my hands, squared my shoulders, and studied the Basics and Beginnings worksheet, the same way I had that day. I ran my pen down the page, noting each of the numbered points. Starting with our dialogue about baptism, I read every word out loud while replicating the gestures:

"I thought of baptism as a way of choosing God in a public way, though it still felt as if I was betraying my Father Abraham." Abandoning him, my childhood idol. My muscles tensed.

"People come to church for many reasons. It's not for me to judge." Pastor's words both reassured and encouraged. I sensed the paradigm shift, reached into the heart of danger, and for a brief moment grasped the truth about my split self, resulting in immediate insight.

I called myself a Christian but was not. I was a prodigal and a fake.

"But I got the sacrament all wrong." My voice shook. I couldn't sit still. Maybe I'd gotten everything wrong. I dropped the pen and paper in my lap. My hands leaped into the air as if by their own volition. "I don't know anything about the New Testament. I don't know anything about Jesus Christ. I don't understand sin. I don't understand suffering."

I took a deep breath and wailed like a child. "I want my comfort back!"

Comfort. I rocked my head to the side. Huh. I hadn't meant God's peace in Christ. Instead of true repentance, I wanted to pity myself and hide behind my angry, lying, accusing, defending inner voice. The voice of Folly. Instead of forgiveness, I wanted comfort, the comfort of control.

The comfort of guilt.

"The comfort of guilt," I said aloud. My shadow's hiding place. "Huh." I rubbed my chin.

I could not admit my sins, let alone die to sin, because I would have to give up control. Choosing guilt allowed me to remain in perpetual internal penitence, judging myself and others, while giving me a false sense of agency over helplessness and suffering. If I chose repentance, I'd have to give up that comfort and accept that suffering is about being human. But if I opened my heart to Jesus's suffering on the cross, in my child's mind, I would betray my mother's sacrificial blood, shed in 1957.

Her injury—and mine. There was the stumbling block. The "What" I'd been looking for.

Instead of immediate insight and joy, I felt something deep and layered rise. The possibility of wholeness. Father, Son, and Holy Spirit. The Son, the gaping hole in my faith.

I bowed my head. "Please, Lord Jesus, help me surrender guilt and receive your mercy. I want to know you, and I can't do any of this on my own."

One giant step forward.

The next Sunday after early service, Keith and I joined the line for coffee in the Fellowship Room before Bible Study. While he chatted with other members of the congregation gathered near the refreshment table, I made my way across the front of the room with coffee cup in hand to claim two empty chairs.

Pastor Tim stood next to the podium, organizing his notes for class. He looked up and caught my eye. "Hi, Carole, how's it going?"

I felt a slow smile soften my face. "Funny you should ask." I wondered if he'd noticed a difference in me. "I think I've figured something out."

I told him about the comfort of guilt.

"Isn't it strange that I would prefer guilt to forgiveness?"

Pastor's face mirrored my slow smile. "Many people do."

"But it seems so simple, so obvious." I flipped my free hand palm up and shrugged my shoulders. "How come I couldn't see it?"

"You weren't ready."

"And now I am."

"And now you are."

I felt my body relax. "Thank you for your patience. I also want to thank you for addressing the tough issues in your messages and Bible studies. It takes courage—and clarity."

"I appreciate your encouragement. My hope is that they get us thinking, praying, and seeking the Lord. I'm thankful they have been a blessing to you." From one seed sower to another, I thought, only this time I was the girl with China doll eyes.

While I was talking with Pastor, Keith found two seats together. I lowered myself into the folding chair next to him. I was not comfortable sitting on the hard metal chair. Forgiveness is a process. After years of hiding my sins, learning to repent and let go of guilt would take time. And when the wind rattled my house on bad nights, I'd become anxious, my insides panting and pacing like Heathcliff. But I felt comforted all the same, because I was on the right path, God's path for me.

The Sunday morning after my breakthrough, we sang the Agnus Dei, which I'd sung many times in high school and college choirs, before Communion while teaching at Ursuline Academy and Notre Dame Preparatory School, and now in church.

Lamb of God, you take away the sin of the world; have mercy on us.
Lamb of God, you take away the sin of the world; grant us your peace.
Grant us your peace.

I didn't know what I was singing because I didn't want to know. Every moment is a choice. Now I sang with confidence, like a person who'd found her voice. When I walked to the altar, I kept my eyes on the cross. Not Mother's broken and bloody body, her sacrifice for us girls, but Jesus, the Lamb of God, his willing sacrifice, the enormous, unimaginable, paradoxical blessing of blood shed to set all of us free.

After receiving Communion in fellowship, I returned to my seat and offered prayers for others. Grace. Though far from understanding the mystery, I no longer struggled during Communion. Mercy. A weight had lifted because I'd chosen spiritual freedom and hope without abandoning the love of my mother or my father. And at the next infant baptism, I cried tears of joy.

Grace and Mercy. Two unimaginably large steps forward.

Chapter 38

Still the Laundry

I jumped out of the Subaru and ran across the parking lot of our local bank to greet my children, stepping out of a rental car. When I saw Jessica glance at David and his partner, my heart knew she'd be unhappy if she didn't get the first hug. She wore skin-tight leather pants, a generous amount of makeup, and yellowish-white spiked hair. In recent months on Facebook, I had seen pictures of her hair dyed blue then pink.

"Merry Christmas, Jessica." I gave her a hug and kiss, which she returned. Did I see relief in her face? "Thanks for coming, Sweetheart."

I turned to David, and we hugged and kissed. He wore jeans and a T-shirt. "May I hug you, too?" I asked his like-clad partner. In the back of the Subaru, Heathcliff and Freya whined and yipped in excitement.

"The mountain road can be tricky, and it's getting dark," I said to David who was driving. "Follow me; it'll only take five minutes. I'll show you where to park."

At the house, they carried their bags upstairs to the loft then settled in the great room. We sipped wine and munched on crackers with homemade salmon mousse. The meat-lovers chili I'd cooked for supper simmered on the stove in the open kitchen.

We sat at the dining table and linked hands. I lifted up a prayer of thanksgiving for safe travels, our family gathering, and good fellowship. Conversation buzzed while we ate, mostly tales from childhood and Christmases past. I'd anticipated my adult children's friendly rivalry.

Toward the end of the meal, David teased his sister about breaking curfew during her rebellious youth. "Your and Mom's shouting was really loud." Both my children laughed. In retrospect, I wish I had laughed, too, or just let the whole thing pass without comment. But to my ears, the laughter sounded like derision.

My gut stirred, but I stayed in my head. "I never understood why you couldn't get home on time, Jessica."

"Oh, Mom, you're such a rule-follower." My mouth opened, but no words came out.

"So am I." Perhaps David wanted to defuse what he'd started. Or maybe he wanted to win. Or maybe the conversation was just all in fun, for them.

But not for me. I lowered my head. "I would think you too would be a rule-follower, Jessica, given your profession."

"Oh no, I know how to break the rules, and I make my own. That's why I'm a lawyer."

Heat flashed through my body. I snapped at the bait. "That's why I pray you have a child. Just. Like. You." The laughter around the table sounded as tight as my clenched fists.

One step back.

"That's not a prayer, that's a curse." Keith's quiet words, meant for me, audible to all.

I sighed and rose from the table. "Would anyone like dessert?"

Throughout Jessica's short visit, I felt guarded and tense, afraid I'd lash out again, especially when we were alone. She had wanted to see her grandma at the assisted care facility, so I arranged a day trip for us while David and his partner went sightseeing. As traffic thinned south of Lynchburg on 29, I asked her how things were going now that she was working in Hong Kong. A safe question, or so I thought.

"Good, I like Hong Kong, but it's been quite painful at times to realize I no longer have a place I can call home." I heard her words of loss but focused on keeping my mouth shut, choosing safety over danger—again. Did she still think it was my responsibility to provide a place for her?

"It's also been liberating." Freedom again. Both-And.

"I'm glad you're making a home for yourself, Jessica. One way or another, we all must. Leaving home is part of life."

In the silence that followed, I remembered the first time I had drawn that "leave home" line and stuck to it. One day, soon after Keith and I returned from her law school graduation weekend, Jessica called out of the blue, asking to live with us for the summer while she studied for the New York bar exam. My heart wanted to say yes, absolutely yes, and my head did, too. I wanted to support her in ways I perceived my father had not supported me, and help her out financially. But my gut knew our time together would not be a Hallmark movie, because I had not brought the tension between us into the light—or my enabling. When I told Keith about her request, he said it wasn't a good idea. We both knew why. If Jessica stayed with us, I'd put Keith in the backseat while I did the driving, and Jessica rode shotgun. It was time to put my marriage first. The next morning, I returned her call, clutching the receiver in a death grip.

"No, Jessica. Our place is small, and Keith and I have a lot on our plates right now with both of us working and me still commuting." I swallowed hard. "Also, you and I do not live well together." A consequence of my need to protect and rescue. A consequence of my failure to set boundaries. A consequence of my not loving her well. Doing love instead of Being love. Why?

"You've made it crystal clear I'll have to fend for myself." I heard the anger. She is her mother's daughter.

"I know you'll figure it out, Jessica." I said, "I love you," hung up the phone, and cried. How to fix this? Again, praying for help never occurred to me, even though it was crystal clear I couldn't do anything by myself. And yet here I was again, driving with Jessica riding shotgun on the way to see my mother.

As I drove the familiar route to the care facility where she lived, "Think, Carole, think," echoed in my head. Father Abraham's words now mine. Eventually, Jessica broke the silence and asked what I was writing. I didn't have enough perspective to explain my fall upward yet but knew how the fall had started.

"Well, for one thing, I've been trying to get to know Keith's daughter."

Jessica interrupted. "I don't get it, Mom, I mean I really don't. I'm your daughter."

"Of course, you're my daughter. I'm writing about you, too. I'll show you some day."

I wasn't ready to tell her about our connections with Gretchen either. Instead, I said, "What I'm really doing is puzzling about who I am now that I've made changes in my life. I'd like to share the lessons I've learned and succeed as a writer."

"Oh Mom, you and success. You're a wife." Her words sounded like indictments. We lapsed into silence again, two miserable women. At least I was, and I imagined she was unhappy, too. How had our relationship come to this, and what to do about it?

During our visit with Mother, Jessica's "wife" comment plagued me. I was happy in my marriage to Keith, so why did I feel as if being a wife made me less than enough? Didn't I know who I was? Why was I afraid to talk with my daughter? This was ridiculous. What was going on?

I had started this journey with my stepdaughter and the Chinese proverb about going into the heart of danger to find safety. Now the journey had led me to my own daughter and another old Chinese proverb: After enlightenment, there is still laundry.

Coming to faith does not make everything different or better or easy. And the blessing of insight does not protect one from suffering. Quite the opposite.

Two and a half years after our initial meeting, I was back in Pastor Tim's office. We sat across from one another at the small table, as we had during our second meeting. Light reflecting off the snow outside the windows cast the room in dazzling white.

"Thanks for taking time to visit with me again," I said.

"I'm happy to meet with you. So, what's happening?"

"In the past few months, I seem to have turned another corner, surrendering more distance. It's new territory for me, much less anxiety, which is an incredible blessing, but not without challenges. I could use your guidance."

"I read the pieces you sent and like the direction you're going."

"Thanks, I think I'm making progress. I've identified what I want more than anything, for myself and others. Success."

"So do I." Pastor rolled his eyes. "Every Sunday, I want my message to succeed. I have to remind myself that what I say is not for my glory but for God's."

I nodded and chuckled. Then I looked down at the blank paper and pen I'd placed in front of me. "I also discovered something else: There are many ways to kill yourself. I don't mean suicide; I mean a living death—killing your Self with a capital S."

Pastor leaned forward and folded his hands on the table. "We kill ourselves by denying God. He loves us the most, and we push Him away."

I scribbled notes as fast as I could.

"We need to ask in what ways do I push the Lord away? How do I hold Him ransom? How do I reward myself with these activities?"

"Walls. I construct them against God so I can control the terrible fear and anger I've felt since Mother was hurt, and to prevent panic attacks." I stopped to think about what I had said. "I also build walls against those who might hurt me. Because when others push my buttons, I lash out as if I want to kill their Selves instead of mine." This time I paused to remind myself of the truth. Sometimes I lash out when things don't go the way I want them to, according to my will. Anger that leads to killing innocent grasshoppers, what I'd learned about myself that day.

I swallowed the knot of anxiety in my throat and told Pastor the real reason for my visit.

"I'm worried about my daughter. She was so unhappy during her Christmas visit, unhappy with me. And she keeps changing the color of her hair. If she acts like this at work, I'm afraid she'll lose her job." I saw Pastor blink and knew I'd taken a step back but kept talking. "All during her visit, I was afraid I'd get angry, so I tried not to say anything."

"Not saying anything can be as damaging as saying something."

Oh Lord, the AA/Al-Anon Serenity Prayer: "God, grant me the serenity to accept the things I cannot change, the courage to change the things I can, and the wisdom to know the difference." I needed to accept what I could not change and change what I could—me.

Pastor placed his hands flat on the table and stretched back, giving us both time to think. Then he leaned forward and folded his hands again. "I have a suggestion, and it's going to sound weird. Try praying scripture. It'll seem like you're reading God's words back to Him. But scripture will help align your prayers with His truth."

After our meeting, I prayed scripture out loud every morning, using references from the devotional blogs I followed, and soon discovered the obvious: I was far from God's truth. Maybe my misalignment showed up in my new writing class, too, because a classmate, a long-time recovering alcoholic, recommended I revisit the AA/Al-Anon Twelve Steps. One morning at home, I took my classmate's advice. To paraphrase, Step One: I admit I am powerless, and my life is unmanageable. Check. Step Two: I believe a power greater than me can restore me to sanity. Check. Step Three: I've made the decision to turn my will and life over to God.

Trust. Um, maybe not.

In truth, I was pre-Step One. I did not want to admit powerlessness. As a prodigal—my first lesson from the parable—I wanted things to happen to my satisfaction. As a dutiful rule-follower, my second lesson, I wanted to earn love and win attention. In both cases, I wanted control, which meant denying God and killing my Self. To accept God's grace and mercy, I would have to humble myself, turning my will and life over to a power greater than me. But I did not want to trust and certainly didn't want anyone shining a light on my shortcomings. I preferred to hide my sins in a dark closet and cling to my comforting whack-a-mole guilt.

I pushed away from my desk and prayed palms up. *Dear Lord, please help me let go of resentments and fears. Please humble my pride. Help me be honest, thoughtful, and most of all loving. Help me let go of guilt and make amends when I see Jessica next time without making a mess or expecting anything from her. Please stay close to her. In Jesus's name, I pray. Amen.*

God must have heard my prayer because the Spirit guided me to Step One.

Chapter 39

I am Powerless.

I should not have been surprised when the answer to my prayer for humbled pride took place in writing class. The pieces we shared were personal, from the heart. Over the years in various groups, I'd developed a sense of professional distance—it's about the work, not the person—and felt more-or-less comfortable in this community. But the day "Step One" distance closed, I was both uncomfortable and furious, as I had been years ago after deciding to believe in God.

Our instructor had given us an assignment to write a scene that combined the dark side and joy. I went into the heart of danger and wrote about my father's burial—the darkness and what had brought us joy. When asked to share our pieces, I volunteered to read first. It's about the work, not the person. I lifted the cover of my laptop and read:

We stood graveside, my children and I with Mother, my sisters Jane and Leslie, Daddy's nine siblings, some with spouses, a few of my cousins, and longtime family friends Dr. and Mrs. Taffel. No funeral, only burial, maybe a memorial—later. That's what Mother wanted.

"Your father thought he'd never die," she'd said. Surely the God he didn't believe in would make an exception. Even while she took care of him during his decade-long illness, Daddy hadn't stated his final wishes.

Yet back in the 60s, long before the inevitable seemed possible, my parents had purchased two side-by-side plots. Perched on a rise at the edge of the cemetery, they would keep watch over the other graves, both old, dating back to the 1700s, and new. Northwest Cemetery, on the corner of Peck Hill and Seymour Road, owned by the Town of Woodbridge and located three minutes from my parents' home.

Did I hear cars or trucks pass the cemetery entrance on that clear, warm day in late June, the day we buried Daddy? I don't remember, only the smell of fresh-mown grass and pine trees. And dirt.

Eight of Daddy's siblings spoke a few words, but not his oldest brother. He paced and grimaced, an expression he and my father shared. I chewed the inside of my mouth and tasted the fear of what my uncle might say. Would he spew jealousy, that his brother born the year after him had upstaged him yet again? Or grief for ignoring what he and Daddy both knew stood between them? Something that also ran in the family.

Unforgiveness.

Tears stung my eyes. "I can't do this." I slapped the laptop away from me. Furious for weeping in front of my colleagues. Furious for losing control. Furious for not being able to hide my angry, pitiful self.

I bowed my head. This was not about the work; this was the humbling. What might I see in my classmates' faces if I looked up? Pity? Disapproval? I couldn't bear the thought. Breaking the silence, my writing buddy asked if I wanted her to finish reading my piece. I nodded—wordless. She angled my laptop toward her and read:

I glanced at Dr. and Mrs. Taffel. In his late 80s and frail, Dr. Taffel leaned on his wife of over fifty years. She, like my mother, would outlive her husband.

"If you gotta exit, it's extremely fine to see some coming in the entrance," Daddy wrote to me upon the birth of my daughter Jessica, his first grandchild. He understood exiting. As a pediatrician teaching in a city hospital and specializing in neonatal intensive care, he saw people exit every day including the very young. He wept for those wee babies and their families. But on the day Jessica made her entrance, he wept for joy.

Sixteen years later, Jessica stood on my right, her twelve-year-old brother David on my left, the three of us hand-in-hand, standing graveside. My two joys each held a long-stemmed rose in their free hands, red roses to place upon their grandfather's coffin.

"Goodbye, Grandpa," we said.

That is what my mother wanted.

My writing buddy angled the laptop toward me, and I shut the cover. Still the laundry. After all these years, I had not mourned my father, a stumbling block too big for me, as Gretchen's journals had been at first reading. Both fear of betraying and abandoning my Father Abraham and grudge at his perceived betrayal and abandonment had blocked my mourning. Again, distance and anger had protected me from suffering and thus prevented the healing.

"I don't know anything about the New Testament. I don't know anything about Jesus Christ. I don't understand sin. I don't understand suffering," I'd said in Pastor's office. Now I understood that suffering goes hand-in-hand with growth and connects us with others and to God. Now I understood we all carry past hurts, even when we don't know it, and if we suffer well, darkness yields to the light. Joy. Now I understood my father's "God is dead, there is no God" outburst as helplessness in the face of children suffering. This, from a man who never had a childhood. On the day his father, my grandfather, lost his right foot and part of his leg in a farm accident, my father became a man—at the age of five. Another connection I hadn't wanted to see, except my father saw the blood, the terrible trail of blood. Now I understood his anger, his need to be a star, to earn love, the jealousy and unforgiveness.

I am my father's daughter, and I'm going to have to learn how to suffer and forgive and ask and wait and trust.

After class, I thought about the sentence in my piece repeated at the end: what my mother wanted. The words referred to a letter Mother had written to us three daughters the year before Daddy died. Written on a dreary, unhappy day after an unhappy-thinking week, she admitted.

"I want to express my desires at my death," she wrote. What Mother wanted for herself. No funeral or memorial. Her daughters and grandchildren could see her to her final resting place. "I'd like someone to say the 23rd Psalm and the Lord's Prayer and whatever else you choose to say. I'd like one red rose from each of the adults and a white rose from the grandchildren. If some of you find it impossible to come, be sure that I've taken a host of memories with me."

Only God knew if she would take those memories with her. God willing, I would pray the Lord's Prayer and recite the 23rd Psalm as she walked through the valley of the shadow of death. What my maybe-there-is-and-maybe-there-isn't Mother wanted, I would do with joy.

But I knew the piece I'd shared was not about my parents but about our humanity. I had written about darkness and joy, the both-and of unforgiveness and forgiveness, knowing I needed to forgive not by practicing or pretending but by admitting I could not extend grace and mercy to anyone by myself. I needed to empty myself and accept this "being" truth.

Step One: I am powerless.

After two-and-a-half years, I sat more comfortably in Bible study, a community of Christian women of various denominations. On Tuesday mornings, we gathered in an old farmhouse owned by one of the members. One morning, after opening prayer, our teacher began her lesson by saying, "According to N.T. Wright, we need to understand first-century Jewish culture, so we don't treat people in the twenty-first century as if they are first-century people, and vice versa." As a historian, I felt right at home.

We had studied the Old Testament, starting with the Pentateuch—the first five books also called the Law—then history, wisdom or devotions, and the prophets, both minor and major. Each lesson included references to New Testament passages. Now for the New Testament itself. I scribbled copious notes, which I later transcribed into a document. After checking scripture references, I emailed the file to others upon request. Sharing my gifts. That I could do.

At the end of the lesson, before prayer requests and closing prayer, our teacher said, "Stories are always an index of the worldview of a country." Stories are also an index of our personal worldview, I thought, and my worldview needed a lot of revision. As the women calmly requested prayers for health issues—in family, friends, neighbors, and themselves—for family disputes, for children and grandchildren needing employment or protection, for help with life adjustments, I held my tongue. After falling apart in writing class, I had become guarded. I did not know the women well, so I chose safety. In truth, I did not want to reveal my less-than-perfect life, though I knew someday I'd go into that danger and make a mess of it.

For me, community was still about "doing" not "being." How little I understood God's grace and mercy. I was so undeserving, so mean-spirited to those who hurt me, or I imagined hurt me. How could I be forgiven? But slowly I was learning we all struggle to hold our angry, pitiful, anxious selves together, and we all think we can hide our unflattering qualities. One consequence of denying my true self was thinking I was the only messy one. As Pastor had said, "Guilt drowns us in self-centeredness, pity, and worry." Guilt's nurses offer false comfort and distract us from loving ourselves and others for who we are, both sinners and saints. For many, me included, the comfort of guilt is a constant lure.

I AM POWERLESS.

I had told the women about being an atheist for the first half of my life, perhaps to explain why I sat in silence during prayer requests. I'm ashamed to admit I did not always remember the women's requests in my prayers. Personal prayer still made me uncomfortable, let alone inviting others' suffering in and sharing that which lay heavy on my heart. So, instead of embracing the unity in the community and the privilege of suffering with and praying for others, I defaulted to distance. I chose intellectual comfort rather than emotional connection. All the while, I wholeheartedly believed God would restore me to sanity if I stayed on the path, showing up every week, studying the Word, and praying in a community of believers.

Step Two: I believe.

While I pondered the enormity of forgiveness, spring came to Vanaprastha. One day in early May a FedEx truck drove up the driveway, and the driver handed me a large box filled with beautiful fresh roses and lilies. "Happy (early) Mother's Day!" the card read. "Dave and I wanted to ensure your flowers arrived in plenty of time for you to enjoy them on your much-deserved day. We both miss and love you! Love, Jess and Dave."

Jessica never forgot my birthday or Mother's Day or Christmas or any other holiday, and always included her brother. Keith's words rang in my ears: "The good Gretchen did should be remembered because she gave us all she had." The good, I thought, remember the good because Jessica gives all she has. And it's enough. More than enough. So, what was my problem? Another "What."

While cutting stems and placing the flowers in a vase, I asked myself a series of questions. Did I still fear for my daughter? Yes, obviously. Did I still get angry about the past? Yes, quite apparently. Was I still afraid of being alone? My biggest fear during my college breakdown—alone. Where had that come from? My body, mind, and heart jolted. Of course, from another of Mother's bad-day, kitchen-table stories, one told rarely and only in hushed tones: "My mother and Aunt Edna were illegitimate; their father never claimed them, and their mother abandoned them."

Another secret. Then I remembered Mother standing in the breezeway door, saying, "Don't rebel, don't rebel," before I left home. Not the worry in her spoken words but what I had heard in my head that day. *Don't leave me, please, don't leave me.*

Alone. Abandoned, as Grammy and Aunt Edna had been. As my mother feared the day she was assaulted. Fear of being alone, hiding in plain sight under a blanket of silence. The answer to another "What." Why I couldn't "leave it." Why I couldn't let Jessica go.

I am my mother's daughter. She is her mother's daughter. Three and maybe four generations of fear. That would add weight to Jessica's longing for a home, though she'd moved halfway around the world, and explain why she became angry when she didn't get what she wanted. Fear. Flight. Fight.

As I inhaled the scent of sweet lilies and placed the vase in the great room, I remembered scripture from Bible study. *See how the flowers of the field grow... If that is how God clothes the grass of the field... will he not much more clothe you... do not worry about tomorrow, for tomorrow will worry about itself.* Who's in control? Not me. Thy will, not mine.

Step Three: Thy will be done.

For the rest of my life, I knew I'd have to revisit those three steps. Every. Single. Day.

I am powerless. I believe. Thy will be done. Amen.

Chapter 40

Freedom

On a Sunday morning in early June, I drove to church with Keith as usual. The sun shone across the Rockfish Valley, illuminating a picture-perfect day. Rounding a curve, we saw a squirrel, darting back and forth in the middle of the road. I slowed and held steady so as not to confuse the frightened creature with sudden moves.

"Please," I said. "Please no." At the last moment, the squirrel ran under the driver's side tire. The car shuddered, and we heard the sickening thump. In my rear-view mirror, I saw the squirrel's body, bloody and broken, lying in the road. I had killed a squirrel.

In church, I thought about how people usually don't intend to do harm. Accidents happen. Carl Wilson might have considered his crime an accident. "Hunting, just killed a squirrel," he'd told the two neighbor boys. At his arraignment, he'd pleaded innocent to "disabling a member of the body with intent to maim." My mother surprised him, he said, and he panicked.

He pleaded guilty to assault with intent to rob, a crime that carried a maximum sentence of five years. The newspaper reported, "...psychologists found Wilson to be subject to 'aggressive impulses' which the defendant cannot suppress and must allow to spend themselves out." His defense counsel stated, "The case had 'no reasonable explanation' since Wilson had a happy home life with a wife and a 14-month-old child, was a steady worker with a good job record, and had no financial difficulties." Both-And.

As I remembered it, Carl Wilson was asked to leave the state after his release from prison but didn't stay out of trouble and died a violent death. This might or might not be true, my child's memory being what it is. Fabricated fears—had he sexually assaulted Mother, too—and fears minimized: he won't come back and hurt my mother ever again. I didn't find any further information about Carl Wilson; the case happened too long ago, state and local authorities told me. No matter. A Carl or Carla or some face-slapping bully could show up anytime or anywhere to hurt my children, mother, husband, neighbors, friends, students, dogs, puppies, or me.

I live with that powerlessness—we all do. We live with the insanity of a broken world.

On the way home from church, Keith and I didn't see any sign of the squirrel's body—likely snatched by a turkey vulture or another scavenger. That's nature's way. I felt sad about what had happened but not guilty. When faced with a bad-worse decision, I had chosen bad over worse: killing a squirrel instead of swerving and risking our lives and others.

But I was guilty of the attempted murder of an innocent grasshopper all those years ago. Maybe my attempt succeeded, and my father spared me the truth. Was that a bad choice or worse? What decision would I have made as a parent?

I'm able to ask those questions now. When I shine a light on my true imperfect self, the darkness of anger, guilt, shame, and fear shrinks. But my old behavior patterns are a confusing mess of wants, defaults, and fears. That's what happened with Jessica last Christmas. I wanted love on my terms and forgot forgiveness. Perhaps these are humanity's defaults because when we're afraid, we're all willing to run over others to get what we want.

I pulled the Subaru into our garage, took the keys out of the ignition, and turned to Keith. "I've been thinking about the squirrel I killed and the grasshopper and the decisions we make in life—good, bad, or worse. As you say, there's always another layer of meaning deeper in the onion." Always another puzzle piece to lift up to see a different picture underneath. And asking questions—doubting if you will—is part of the mysterious process of bringing truth to light. Searching, inquiring, making connections, keeping relationships alive, and being for one another.

Keith nodded and smiled. "That's right, always another layer deeper in the onion."

For Labor Day weekend, Jessica had invited me to join her stateside in New York City—her treat for my sixty-fifth birthday. We shared a fabulous hotel room she'd reserved using travel points, sampled new foods at neighborhood restaurants, soaked up inspiration at art museums, and took in another Broadway show. I relished my time with her.

On Saturday afternoon, we walked around Battery Park City, the area devastated by the 9/11 collapse of the World Trade Center. Families and businesses had returned along with trees planted in hope for peace. The day was clear, warm, and breezy, much like the weather during our walk in Connecticut four years before.

As we strolled arm-in-arm, watching joggers, young lovers, parents, children, and old people, I remembered the third person in the parable of the prodigal son, the father, waiting for his child to come home, as I had, as my father had. God's love is steadfast. He shows us His grace every moment of every day and forgives without anger or blame. The parable's third lesson is the third way. Grace. Which did I want to mirror, His grace or human selfishness?

I turned to Jessica. "When you came to visit me at Grandma's house, I tried to make amends. But I made a mess of it. I'd like to try again."

She stopped and squared her shoulders.

"I'm sorry, Jessica, I was not a perfect parent." *Mistakes Were Made.* No but, no blame, no self-defense. No neediness and No More Guilt. I could not give her the freedom or the home she wanted, because they rest not in doing but in being who God wills us to be.

"Thank you." Her voice was gut-low and hard. She is my daughter after all.

Atonement neither changes the past nor removes the consequences of our choices. After a lifetime of living in fear, running from the past, denying my true self, and passing the same along to my daughter, an honest, grace-filled relationship with her would take time and patience. Practice. Building new defaults based on connection, heartfelt love, and forgiveness. Moving toward maturity by holding the tension of both sinner and saint together. The third way. I could not be a perfect mother, but I could be a good one. And the best gift I could give her? My healing-heart.

We walked in companionable peace. Jessica took a selfie of us together, head-to-head with the harbor in the background. Later she posted the picture to Facebook and wrote, "A very special thanks to *Carole Duff* for coming up to spend a fabulous weekend in the city—lots of love for my mom today."

I replied, "Always lots of love for my daughter Jessica, always."

The train to Charlottesville carried few passengers on Sunday afternoon. I read most of the way home. Toward the end of the trip, I lowered my iPad and stared out the window at scenes rushing past: industrial wastelands and residential backyards with derelict vehicles, cracked cinder blocks, and cast-off belongings, detritus people might wish to hide and forget.

In the brokenness, I recognized my own. A weathered toybox—my childish need for winner-take-all attention. A soiled Little Golden Book—my beastly wrath. Scattered paper—my test scores, report cards, and grades—earned-love trophies of meaningless success. An empty doghouse—my faithless anxiety.

Backyard brokenness rumbled on. My never-enough greed, fear of disapproval, angry blame, poor-me self-pity, distance-and-love blindness, self-righteous deafness, silent sulking, I'm-too-smart-to-believe-in-God arrogance, unforgiving grudge. The comfort of guilt. Pride.

This time I didn't reach for any of it. Instead, I prayed palms up and asked for the quiet hum, God's gift to those who turn to Him. Every moment has that choice. I knew when tested I would choose my defaults more often than not—my needy, rebellious, "more me, less Jesus" reflex. Maybe someday I would catch myself in the act and laugh then gently say, "Leave it. You don't need those defaults, not anymore."

Both sinner and saint. The choice to accept myself as I am: both imperfect and a child of God. Who I am and who I choose to be. Being—what God wanted from the beginning. Being—what I'd been waiting for. Being—the "What" I didn't know anything about. Since I still defaulted to "doing everything all by myself," "wanting love on my terms," and "forgetting forgiveness," I knew my journey in faith had only just begun. With that insight, I made the paradigm shift and stepped out of my fall's liminal space into the light, the place where Jesus's great sacrifice redeems us, changes our hearts, the place where mercy overcomes our human quest for power, the place where God's perfect grace resides. The place where Wisdom has built her house, the place where I choose to live.

As the train pulled into the station, I saw the love of my life standing on the platform. Keith took my duffel bag and gave me an oh-my-goodness kiss.

On the way to the car, he said, "I brought Freya. Just before it was time to leave to pick you up, Heathcliff ran off after some critter. I waited as long as I could." He must have seen concern wash across my face. "I left the house and deck lights on. Don't worry. Heathcliff will be there when we get home."

Maybe he will and maybe he won't, I thought.

Freya pressed her nose against the back window then wedged her head out the side window. Her tail wagged her entire body. When I rubbed her head the way she liked, she lifted her muzzle and licked my hand with her pink, black-spotted tongue.

"Good girl, Freya, good girl. I'm happy to see you, too, baby girl."

Keith navigated the Subaru onto the highway and headed west. The Blue Ridge Mountains came into view as night fell across the Rockfish Valley. I prayed palms up in silence again and gave my worry to God. Thy will be done. Your hopes and dreams are far bigger, far better than mine. I will wait because waiting is hope, and I will trust because trusting is faith.

"Did you have a good time?" Keith asked. "We missed you."

"It was a wonderful visit, and I missed you, too." I ran my hand down the back of his head to the nape of his neck. He chuckled, and Freya thumped her tail.

I gazed at the stars in the twilight sky. Our tiny part of the universe, which God created by breathing his Spirit in wind and words. Bright sun during the day, star trails visible at night.

We're going home to Vanaprastha, I mused, to sentinel oaks and forest creatures, turtles and toads, deer, spiders, and lizards roaming the land and hawks floating the thermals, to rock outcroppings and mountain laurel, to narcissus, hibernating each fall under leaves at the base of Gretchen's tree and blooming every spring. Someday, when God's purpose for me is done, I'll let go of everything and return to the earth from which I was made. But tonight, I am living here, now, and I choose to accept this precious moment no matter what happens.

As we drove up the driveway, I saw Heathcliff, standing on the deck.

Waiting.